LIVING THROUGH PERSONAL CRISIS

Ann Kaiser Stearns, Ph.D.

9 April 2012

With Best Wishes,

Ann Kaiser Stearns

Idyll Arbor, Inc.

Idyll Arbor, Inc.

39129 264th Ave SE, Enumclaw, WA 98022 (360) 825-7797

ISBN: 9781882883875

Printed in the United States of America

Most of the names in this book have been changed and, in most cases, the identities of the persons whose stories are told have been disguised in order to protect the confidentiality and sacredness of friendship and of the counseling relationship.

Library of Congress Cataloging-in-Publication Data

Stearns, Ann Kaiser.
  Living through personal crisis / Ann Kaiser Stearns.
      p. cm.
  Originally published: Chicago, Ill. : Thomas More Press, c1984.
  Includes bibliographical references.
  ISBN 978-1-882883-87-5 (alk. paper)
  1. Bereavement--Psychological aspects. 2. Deprivation (Psychology) 3. Life change events. I. Title.
  BF575.G7S74 1984
  155.9'3--dc22

                                                2010002500

In memory of my mother,
Margaret O. Kaiser
And to honor my daughters
Amanda Asha and Ashley Anjali

CONTENTS

To the ancient Egyptians
the phoenix was a legendary bird, consumed by fire,
who rose up from its own ashes
and assumed a new life.
From our own ashes
we also must recreate ourselves, our lives.

— *Ann Kaiser Stearns*

PREFACE TO THE FIRST EDITION

This book is about the small and large losses that happen to people, experiences that plunge them into a period of adjustment. It is for those of you who are moving through a mourning process and for those who are struggling with depression and other symptoms of distress, not yet having realized that you are grieving a loss of some kind.

Not so long ago I experienced a period of personal crisis. As part of an almost desperate attempt to get hold of myself, I submerged, double overtime, into my work. My workaholism itself would become a problem later on, but in a mourning process we don't think about such things. We're too busy just surviving in whatever ways we can.

I felt that something had to be learned or gained from the all-encompassing personal turmoil I was going through. My loss was overpowering. I needed a strategy for survival, and my strategy became a program of personal learning. I consumed the grief literature as someone else might have consumed alcohol. I reviewed what my experiences to that point had taught me about coping with life in the face of loss. I wrote stacks of notes on the healing process of persons with whom I had worked in crisis counseling. Always with the person's knowledge and permission, I recorded many of my therapy sessions with men and women struggling with loss. I took advanced courses at several universities.

Most important, I grieved my own grief with friends, with two different therapists over a period of several years, and within the setting of a women's discussion group. As so often is the case with grief, my older unfinished losses were unleashed. While mourning the loss of my husband through divorce, I began to release feelings of loss having to do with my parents, my childhood, and my concept of myself. For the first time in my life I felt the full range of my human emotions: love, hate, anger, sorrow, guilt, fear, shame, self-blame, and, eventually, joy.

Out of all those feelings came a series of lectures on the subject of living through personal crisis. These lectures were presented to young adults, senior citizens, and every age group in between: I spoke to homemakers, office and factory workers, business and professional people, college and graduate students. I also gave numerous presentations to physicians and nurses; ministers, priests, sisters, and rabbis; funeral directors, psychologists, social workers, counselors, and police officers; and to many others in the human service occupations. The response of these hundreds of people made me realize that what I had learned about loss was valuable to many more persons than myself.

This book deals with a subject experienced at some level by almost everybody. I have avoided the technical and clinical language that we professionals in the field and college professors are prone to use. It was important to me that my work be readable by anyone with an interest in understanding loss.

The book is written for the person who is now hurting or who has struggled with troublesome and hurtful feelings in the recent past, as well as for the person's family and friends. Perhaps you are suffering a present loss or an old one never really brought to rest, and you feel powerless to help yourself. Or perhaps a loved one has suffered a loss and you feel uncertain about how to help. You need to understand your loved one's grieving process.

The book was also written for me. Once and for all, I wanted to make peace with my own losses. Unresolved pain keeps us from being complete, content people. Writing this book has helped me to let go of that pain.

Sometimes I think I've managed to come through my own losses because I've been so caught up in trying to understand the grief of others. But it works both ways. I've had to grow more accepting of the craziness, pain, and pride of grief in myself in order to become an effective helping professional. Nobody wants a teacher, therapist, or friend who presents himself or herself as being without vulnerability to suffering. We learn best from people who are human beings.

As a young adult, with my first hospital patients to care for, I sought out the counsel of a beloved professor. Working with gravely ill patients on a university hospital's medical ward had provoked within me a storm of unsettling memories. For several weeks I periodically sat in my professor's office weeping. He was a man with young children and I knew that his wife was dying of cancer, but he listened attentively. Finally, I told Dr. Goodling that I felt guilty speaking of my losses and crying for myself. Surely, I said, his sorrow was more profound than mine. In the years since then, I've quoted many times to my own students my professor's powerful reply. "Don't let my suffering," he said, "rob you of your own."

You may also have to give up the idea that you aren't entitled to mourn because others have greater sorrows. All of us have both the right and responsibility to take our losses seriously. Grief, when ignored or denied, can do us in, harming us in dozens of ways. Facing our losses is part of how we find our freedom again. That's how healing begins.

PREFACE TO THE NEW EDITION

Since I wrote the first edition of this book, everything has changed and nothing has changed. What has changed is that acts of senseless violence worldwide and in America have hit closer to home and taken to new levels both human suffering and courage. The truck-bomb murder of 168 men, women, and children in a government building in Oklahoma City as well as the copycat school shootings and mass killings in churches, synagogues, post offices, and other settings have stunned us with the realization that many evil, destructive deeds occur in unlikely places and even at the hands of homegrown terrorists and troubled teens.

Three thousand innocent people — Americans and citizens of many other countries — tragically lost their lives on September 11, 2001. In the free world, and perhaps more than ever before in the United States, we were united in mourning, compassion, outrage, and resolve.

The wars in Afghanistan and Iraq, with repeated military deployments, have taken an enormous toll in lost lives, disability, and mental illness. Tens of thousands of soldiers have been overexposed to extreme trauma and their families overly exposed to emotional distress and financial hardship. They need and deserve the support of friends, employers, their communities, and government programs and policies.

Since the earlier edition of this book, something else causing pain in millions of people's lives is the expanding prevalence of cyberspace crimes. Sexual predators now use the Internet to prey on countless children while other predators scam, scheme against, or steal the identities of the elderly, the unemployed, and anyone else who is vulnerable. All of these events cause enormous grief and require a long and difficult healing process.

We were shocked by the terrible suffering and loss of life resulting from the Asian tsunami, Hurricane Katrina, and the Haitian earthquake. The worst financial crisis since the Great Depression of the 1930s has threatened many lives in an all-encompassing way — jobs, homes, family, health, and security. As I write these words, our country is experiencing a new surge of hope — but we may suffer through more losses before we can all come to healing.

◊ ◊ ◊

What has not changed is that people still get to the other side of a significant loss or personal crisis only by going *through* it, which is why the title of the book stays the same.

Hurting is a necessary part of everyone's healing, but so is hope, regardless of the nature of your loss. Virtually all of us suffer from some form of depression, have to deal with frustration and angry feelings, struggle with sleep problems or conflicted relationships, experience guilt or self-blame, or all of the above.

In order to build a rewarding life in the aftermath of tragic, disappointing, and painful events, most of us look for coherence. We try to make some kind of sense out of our loss. It's a necessary part of healing that doesn't change.

People survive a personal crisis when they learn something from it. It is never easy. But when we learn to use pain for something redemptive, such as eventually being able to help someone else, our crisis or loss is transformed into something that makes us stronger.

An event leading to what felt like meaningless sorrow or injury can bring hope or healing to someone else. Often it's someone we love dearly whom we are able to help. As time goes on, dozens or even hundreds of people are helped by the lessons burned into us by pain.

Even when you think you don't *want* to learn from tragedy — such as the death of your child or a horrible violent act done by a cruel person — it is still the case that we best honor someone we love and give meaning to our loss when we choose to go forward and refuse to be destroyed.

What hasn't changed is that *Living Through Personal Crisis* still speaks truth and offers hope. Those who are hurting and who yearn to rebuild a fulfilling life will find a healing path here.

A Personal Note

Thanks to the late and influential syndicated columnist Ann Landers, this book became a national bestseller and is now published in seven languages. She repeatedly recommended *Living Through Personal Crisis* and wrote in her column that "Never in all my years of recommending books have so many people written to thank me." She quoted the appreciative words of many readers who were helped by my book in various cities nationwide. I will always be thankful for the doors that flew open after that.

From the time I was a teenager growing up in rural Oklahoma and New Mexico, finding ways to help other people has given meaning to the losses in my own life. Through college teaching, writing books and articles, counseling, interviewing inspirational people, lecturing around the country, or meeting people through radio and television work, I've grown stronger and learned so much from the life stories and healing journeys of others. As you continue to read this book, I hope that you also will feel encouraged and be strengthened in moving forward with your life.

ACKNOWLEDGMENTS

This book was made possible thanks to the very good work and emotional support of Joan Kesselring, freelance editor Ilene McGrath, Sandee Widomski, and Judith Vetter Douglas. Ashley A. Stearns and Dawn F. Reyes helped with the typing. Joanne Munden helped in more ways than I can count. Reverend George Merrill, and Drs. Van Richards, Marilyn Persons, Richard A. Goodling, and David Hobson provided helpful early encouragement and criticism. Norma and Jack Danz, Eleanor and Frank Fink, Naomi and Steven Shelton, Dr. Al Marshello, Marian and Blake Wattenbarger, Margaret and Bill Keys, and other friends were wonderfully supportive, too. I was encouraged to write this new edition by Mark Doyal of Glow Communications, LLC, and supported by my close friends Rev. Keith I. Pohl and Roberta Pohl, Dorris Hoyle, the Wattenbargers, Cherry Marquez, Burt and Linda English, Colonel Kim Ward, Professor Jan Allen, Dr. Janyne Althaus, Dr. J. Raymond DePaulo, Jr., Dr. Donald Slowinski and Val Slowinski, Betty Beall, Charlie Metz, Melissa Hopp, Rev. Mary Gaut, and my department chair, Dr. Tim Davis. My lawyer, Anthony Elia, has contributed the expertise, calm demeanor, and steady support for which any author would be grateful. Also deserving of special thanks are Diane Bliss, Josette Marano, and Jamie Westrick of Detroit Public Television. They recruited and guided me in presenting a PBS program, which they produced, to be aired nationally with this book as one of the gifts to public television contributors. My daughters, Amanda and Ashley, were awesome in giving their love and affection. Our border collie, Panda, was right by my side as well.

1. NOT TO BE AFRAID

The main thing in life is not to be afraid to be human.

— Pablo Casals

Bereavement comes from the word "reave," meaning "to be dispossessed," to be robbed of something belonging to oneself.[1] When a woman has a mastectomy, something is forcibly taken away, a possession rightfully hers. When a man has a heart attack and has to change his way of living and working, something is taken away, choices and decisions that previously belonged to him. When parents lose a child, they are dispossessed of something very precious.

In words that have been attributed to Camus, "The order of nature is reversed. Children are supposed to bury their parents." When people of any age undergo the trauma of war or are otherwise victimized by violence, their sense of safety can never be fully restored. Suffering the ordeal of a divorce or the loss of a loved one by death often leaves one with a sense of having been robbed, dispossessed. Having a miscarriage or finding oneself unable to have children — one can see how these losses also could be experienced as losing something rightfully one's own.

Many other situations can carry a sense of irrevocable injury: rape, betrayal, chronic illness, the birth of a handicapped child, the breakup of a love affair, the loss of a job, abortion, the loss of a dream or goal, the loss of personal belongings in a fire or flood, a major geographical move that involves leaving behind one's roots and friends. There is also, of

1

course, perhaps the ultimate dispossession: facing the loss of one's own life.

There is another kind of grief that many of us encounter. Usually it happens in our 20s or 30s, sometimes later. We begin to realize that our childhood was as it will always be: a broken family, an alcoholic or mentally ill parent, a loved one who died prematurely. Even in the happiest of families there are sorrows of various kinds. Our parents and siblings are as they will be. We can't change them. We can't make them happier, or healthier, or more careful of themselves, or less misunderstanding of us. Grief sets in, for the events of the past are unalterable, and the sense of loss may be experienced as a death.

Life involves almost all of us in losses of significant magnitude. When I was 20, I thought that all of my dreams were capable of being realized. If an older person said I couldn't have it all or control it all, I was insulted. What is clearer now is that there are choices we make and there is the reality that in pursuing some of our dreams we leave other dreams behind. Through both events of our own making and events beyond our control, we come to realize our human vulnerability. It's a realization that none of us likes to face, but it's something we can come to understand.

Grief is not a mental illness. It just feels that way sometimes. If you had all the symptoms of grief but no loss experience that triggered the multitude of your troublesome feelings and behaviors, that would be a different story. In that case, you might need a full psychological and medical examination.

Sleeplessness, anxiety, fear, intense anger, suicidal ideas, a loss of interest in activity, a preoccupation with self and with sad feelings — you may think these all add up to "going crazy." Actually, each of these things can be a part of the grieving process. You probably don't need professional help, just an understanding of the battle you're fighting.

A young woman, soft-spoken and poised, was talking with me. It had not yet been 48 hours since her brother's death by suicide. Theresa seemed older than her 18 years. She was not crying, although an occasional wetness came across her eyes. With extraordinary rationality, Theresa outlined why she wanted to begin counseling. She spoke in a monotone as if reporting a non-newsworthy item on a news program. She had wanted, she said, to overcome her self-destructiveness for a long time. She wanted to learn to take better care of herself; her brother's suicide was a reminder of her own suicidal thoughts in the past. Continuing in a calm voice, Theresa, who had just come from the funeral home, began to speak about her brother. Her strange sense of presence is typical of very early grief. She was in a state of shock. In the first several days our emotions are blunted and the impact of the loss has not been fully experienced.

At first we are apt to move back and forth between a calm frame of mind and tearfulness. We feel bewildered and stunned, although often we are quite capable in manner. We disbelieve what has happened. On awakening in the middle of the night or in the morning, we may wonder for a moment whether our loss really happened.

Gradually, usually within the first six to eight days, increased sadness begins. A depressed mood sets in, a mood that will affect all that we are, think, and do for many months.[2] Years later it may be clear that our loss has transformed us, that a rich process of self-discovery has come from all of this — but for now we battle with depression.

Everything is a reminder of the loss. It's as if a great cosmic conspiracy were in operation, inflicting pain. Television shows, even news programs, remind us of our grief. Other people's conversations, some of them wholly unrelated to our circumstances, intensify our preoccupation with the loss. Songs on the radio play memories across hidden screens behind our eyes. Sometimes we cannot even eat a certain food without remembering the last time a particular meal was before us.

How different were our circumstances then. Strangers on the street, certain automobile models, items of clothing, a hospital or a restaurant or a school that we try to avoid — all of these call out to us as tragic reminders.

If you have lost your marriage partner or lover, you will notice every couple there is to see, hand in hand. Happy people will seem to be everywhere, intensifying your sense of isolation. If you have had a miscarriage or an abortion, every pregnant woman pushing a grocery cart may remind you of what might have been. Every little child or tricycle along the street may speak to you.

If you have lost your health, your career, someone you love, or a part of your body, you will look with resentment at dozens of people who haven't any idea what it is to be in your situation. One of the insanities of grief is that the rest of the world seems to go on thriving while the pulse beat within ourselves feels so deadened.

Our preoccupation with the loss is especially intense in the earlier months. We tend to avoid particular friends or work associates or certain places and experiences. We fear that our once precious but now painful memories will be engulfing. We are afraid of becoming overwhelmed.

When a person has been lost, we are apt to become preoccupied with objects owned, given by, or associated with him or her. There is a great cherishing of things. We may sort through old photos, letters, or other keepsakes — over and over and over. What once brought joy now brings sadness, and sometimes comfort. There is a feeling of conflict within us as we experience both avoidance and cherishing. Certain reminders are painful yet comforting, while other reminders are just too much to bear.

The sorting goes on. You may not want to give away or throw away these objects or possessions for quite a while. Sometimes when we act too quickly we regret it deeply later on. If it will help you to feel better, put some of those things away in an attic or closet. On the other hand, regardless of what others advise you, you needn't put any cherished thing away, not until you feel ready to do so. Your preoccupation is not a sickness. It's part of the normal process of separation.

When a significant loss has us in its grip, a minimum of six months to a year is usually required for healing. Some aspects of the grieving process continue into the second year. Resolution may not come until even later.

If you are recovering from a brain injury or exposure to the violence of war, addiction, criminal acts, or child or spouse abuse, the healing process is apt to unfold over a period of years.

The length of time required for mourning depends largely on the circumstances of the loss. Many who grieve the slow death of a loved one or gradual deterioration of a marital relationship engage in anticipatory mourning. They begin the grieving process long before the relationship with their loved person actually ends. In such a situation, only a few days, weeks, or months of emotional turmoil may follow the loss, since a significant adjustment process has already transpired. On the other hand, when the death of a loved one comes suddenly or when a person is forced to cope with radical surgery, a debilitating accident, or other unforeseen tragedy, the mourning process would be expected to last at least a year.

Younger people often grieve longer and harder when losing a spouse or partner or suffering a shattered dream because the loss is unexpected and greatly disrupts life plans. Most older widows and widowers grieve intensely but do well sooner. They have already reached their primary goals or accepted the reality that some dreams will not come true. Because many of their peers have also lost their partners, older people don't feel as singled out by fate or suffer as much regret.[3]

Family estrangement can also prolong and complicate the grieving process. When a grieving grandparent, gay or lesbian partner, or other family member is denied hospital visitation or prevented from actively participating in the funeral service, the emotional impact can be felt as cruelty. What brings comfort are friends, faith communities, gay and lesbian and other support groups, and alternative memorial services and rituals.[4]

Other factors in the length of time that mourning requires are what the loss means to the person, the personality attributes and coping style of the individual, and who is available to help.[5] One woman may have great difficulty with her decision to have an abortion because of her religious beliefs or ambivalent feelings about wanting a child. If family members or friends condemn her or a troubled relationship exists with the man involved in the pregnancy, or if there are no friends with whom she feels she can share her struggle, she may mourn bitterly for a year or longer. Another woman in different circumstances might feel sorrow and regret but mourn for a far briefer period, perhaps only a few days or weeks. In other situations the loss of a child can take many years to heal, and the bereaved parent may never feel that he or she has fully recovered from the loss.

As a graduate student overseas, I learned that a number of other cultures are considerably more realistic in recognizing the length of time mourning requires. In Cairo I stayed at the home of an Egyptian woman and her brother, both of whom dressed entirely in black for six months following their mother's death. I learned that the Moslem custom is to wear mourning clothes during the entire first year of bereavement. In Israel, the Orthodox Jewish custom is to offer prayers for the deceased parent every day for eleven months and to mourn for twelve Hebrew months. At the time, it seemed to me an awfully long time to mourn. Later, as I began to study grief, this Mideastern custom of a one-year mourning period made a great deal of sense.

In our culture, mourning symbols are seldom worn beyond the day of the funeral. As a child in rural Oklahoma, I saw that black armbands worn for a period of several weeks recognized death. In today's world, flowers and photos or flags, teddy bears, or religious symbols are left at the scene of a terrorist attack, car crash, or school shooting or at the doorstep of a grieving family.[6] Other than lapel ribbons or buttons, we generally lack accepted public symbols of the fact that a grieving person's life does not go on again in a normal way for quite some time. A large gap exists between what we feel and what others seem to expect.

Grief is profoundly misunderstood in American society. A visitor once came to one of my college classes because he heard we were talking about grief. He said he was worried about an uncle who was "not taking his marital separation well at all." The visitor was obviously troubled that his uncle talked almost constantly about his estranged wife and was "still tearful." When asked how long it had been, the well-meaning nephew replied, "Well, it has already been four months!" He had not yet learned that people aren't having emotional breakdowns just because mourning takes a long time. Such unrealistic expectations about the mourning period often lead the mourner to feel anxious, self-doubting, and afraid.

A widower may come home from work at night and open the door to the aroma of his wife's dinner cooking, even though there is nothing being cooked. For many years dinner had been on the stove when he came home. What is real is perceived as an unreality. More vivid to the widower's experience than the absence of his wife are all the years that went before. He is not mentally ill. He is going through what one-fourth to one-third of all bereaved persons experience, especially in the early weeks and months of grief. He is having a hallucinatory experience.

If you ask him, he will tell you that his wife is dead. But he may also tell you that he hears her in the kitchen at night, having gotten out of bed for a midnight snack as she so often did. She is gone, but her memory is vividly present in his mind.

Although some remnants of preoccupation with a loss are more all encompassing in the early months, they can continue to emerge much later. A student of mine was convinced that he saw his father at a baseball game at the stadium in Baltimore more than a year after his father's death. He was greatly relieved to learn that such experiences are quite common to grief. For some years after my divorce, I occasionally waved vigorously at strange men in automobiles on the freeways and streets of Baltimore. At first glance I had believed each of these men to be my former husband, and I longed to talk with him once more! Those whom we have loved or with whom we have unfinished business often remain with us in vivid ways.

A greatly distraught woman in her 50s came to her family physician complaining of having frightening hallucinations. She was afraid she was losing her mind. The woman's 30-year-old daughter had taken her own life with sleeping pills six days before. Since the suicide, the woman had twice seen her daughter come into the house, real as life. The first time, she played music for her mother before departing, as she had come, through the front door. The second time, the daughter came as though she wished to speak to her mother but was unable to.

Because this woman was highly upset by her hallucinatory experiences, her family wisely decided to take her to the family physician. Fortunately, he understood her grief. The woman was not mentally ill. She was suffering two of the most traumatic losses a person can endure: the loss of a child and the loss of a loved one by suicide.

Although profound loss does not usually precipitate mental illness, it can. A person with a previous history of severe depression, anxiety, or a history of other psychiatric illness in the family is especially vulnerable. Mental illness can produce hallucinations, as can a severe grief reaction. For this reason, if the hallucinations persist, a professional consultation is needed. Such a consultation is also urgently recommended if the grieving person gives any indication that he or she is contemplating suicide. The vast and overwhelming majority of grieving persons, it must be emphasized, are not precipitated into mental illness. The widower who heard his wife in the kitchen and smelled her cooking is simply struggling with separation. He knows his wife is dead. He misses her terribly, that's all.

Grieving people go through a very personal healing process, which is referred to by the psychological term *desensitization*. When we first begin to face a traumatic experience or loss, everything is a reminder to us. As time goes on, we reencounter many of these persons, places, objects, and experiences, which initially were quite painful to us. We become desensitized, not hurt as easily. We grow less sensitive, for example, from repeatedly hearing certain songs on the radio. Suppose, though, you do not hear a certain song for two years. When you first hear it after this time, you may again become depressed and sad. Old stimuli that have not yet been encountered in the present have a way of popping up again. Thus the desensitization process can be long and difficult. Once the grieving and healing process has run its course, however, we aren't so vulnerable.

Well-intentioned friends, and even some professionals who ought to know better, may tell you that you have become overly self-centered and self-preoccupied. Usually this reaction is an indication of the speaker's own discomfort with loss and troublesome but human emotions. Self-centeredness is almost always an essential aspect of separating from someone or something precious that has been lost, and so it is a common characteristic of grief. I'm not saying that returning to work or school as soon as possible is not a good idea. It *is* helpful to try to continue the activities of living, even if you have to push yourself in the beginning. But don't expect to be thinking about your work while you're going through these motions of activity. Especially in the early months, your mind will be largely on yourself and on your troubled feelings. As the first months go by, you will probably think of yourself and of your ordeal more than you think about anything else. This preoccupation is not illness, nor is it an indication of weakness or selfishness. It is simply human adjustment in the face of personal crisis. The greater your loss, the more likely and the longer you are to be preoccupied with your own feelings.

Feelings of loneliness and sorrow may be intensified by the happiness of others. Well-meaning friends may attempt to involve you in weddings, parties, and other social events and may expect you to have a happy attitude as well. You may feel guilty that you don't feel like sharing others' good times or good fortune. Nevertheless, it is very important not to isolate yourself from warm human contact and community. You do need activity and the company of friends. But you need not feel ashamed when your thoughts keep returning to yourself, or when you wish to avoid certain activities and social settings. Remember that self-preoccupation is one of the ways we recover and rebuild our lives. Try not to be afraid of your inwardness. It's the beginning of a healing process.

2. THINGS WILL NEVER BE THE SAME

... if dreams die
Life is a broken-winged bird
That cannot fly.
... when dreams go
Life is a barren field
Frozen with snow.

— Langston Hughes

Louise was an attractive woman in her middle 40s. One night after class, as the other students filed out of the room, she stayed behind in her seat, weeping.

Later, in my office, Louise buried her face in her hands. We sat for what seemed a long time without speaking. Watching her tears, I wished that people bringing their problems to me wouldn't feel so ashamed. "Why is allowing me to share your pain so hard for you?" I protested silently. "Why can't you look at me?" Then, as my mind did a little dance through troubled times of mine, I remembered having often hidden my own face in this way. When I was seeking help, a warm and accepting woman doctor used to ask why I wouldn't let her see my face when I cried. Like Louise, I learned as a child to feel embarrassed when unable to solve my own problems. It's okay, I decided. Louise feels she needs right now to cover her face with both hands.

Finally Louise began to speak, still hiding. Her marriage of 25 years was falling apart, she said. And she had learned today that their teenage daughter is using illegal drugs. "All my life I've been a good Catholic," she cried. "No birth control. Four little children all lined up in a row. I

11

never complained. I just kept having children. And I never missed church." She was sobbing. "I've always been good; I've worked at being good. Now look what's happening! Everything is falling apart!"

Louise's crisis was a spiritual one, the kind of assault on our inner sense of fairness that yanks away our illusions. In some way or other, things will never be the same. We come to know, in an overwhelmingly personal way, that we haven't any special immunity to sorrow. Louise was asking from the core of her inner self whether it matters at all how hard a person tries to live a good and decent life. She felt betrayed, she said, not merely by the church's teachings. Somehow, she felt betrayed by God as well.

As I remember Louise, I think how hard it has been for me to learn the same thing: that none of us is immune to suffering. Although spiritually minded in a different way, from time to time I have felt many of the same feelings Louise was struggling with. "Doesn't it matter for anything," I once protested to my friend Judy, "that I've had years of therapy and the best in education? Doesn't that library of books that I own protect me at all? Can I be this busy living a useful life, know as much as I know about human psychology, and *still* be hurt by losses of my own?" My friend's answer, of course, is no surprise to a person working through a grief process. "There aren't any guarantees against sorrow for any of us," she said.

Our losses challenge us and change the course of our lives. It's not that one can never again be happy after an experience of loss. The reality is simply that one can never again be the same.

Once a parent has been lost, he or she is no longer available to share our joys and hurts, our accomplishments and milestones. The milestones can be shared with others, but things are never the same. Always someone will be missing. Intense in the first year, an empty feeling comes and goes for years thereafter. Later on we can experience the important events of our lives in the knowledge that our lost parent is alive within us, but that doesn't alter the fact that everything is different right now.

If a child in the family has been lost, from that day on your family will not be complete. From time to time you will have the thought of how old the daughter or son, brother or sister, would now be, if alive. What would have become of him or her? After a long period of grieving you will find many family joys over the years, but always someone will be missing, and those joys will have to be different ones than would otherwise have been. Things just can't be the same.

One of the most difficult aspects of grief is the loss of potential. A psychologist friend was talking with me about the death of his father. "My father was a truck driver and able to do very little for me financially," Sheldon said. "But when he died, that possibility was never there again, the possibility that he could help me if I needed him."

There is also a sense of regret when a relationship ends before the conflicts of that relationship can be resolved. Always kept alive, even faintly, is the hope of reconciliation as long as the loved one is present. That potential is lost with death, and sometimes with divorce, family dissolution, or other separation. Whatever peace is made must be worked out by the grieving person without the aid of the one who was lost.

When a person suffers a traumatic injury or life-changing illness, is victimized by crime or a natural disaster, gives up a child for adoption, has an abortion, ends a marriage, or suffers the loss of a career, a whole world of potential comes to a halt. What must now be developed is an entirely new life with new self-definitions. This is true of many other loss situations as well.

Human emotions cannot be ordered away from the arena like misbehaving fans at an athletic event. Although the belief that our lives are permanently ruined will not last forever, we do need the time to feel our feelings of ruin fully. After weeks or even months, we can go on.

If you have ever been raped, literally or in some symbolic way, you can never be the same again. It's not that you can't overcome this traumatic experience and your troublesome feelings about it. You can. Still, you have suffered an assault on your dignity. Your experience has made you know in a deeply personal way what it means to be degraded and humiliated. That personal knowledge can't help but change you. Probably you will resent and distrust people for some years. And when you do regain your sense of trust in human decency, you will have been required by life to find strengths inside yourself that were previously unknown to you.

Thousands of men and women periodically ask themselves what their lives might have been without devastating war injuries. When permanent brain injuries or physical impairment must be borne, for whatever reason, everything changes. Debilitating arthritis, the loss of normal sight, hearing, or speech, or losing the use of a part of one's body because of a stroke or other injury — each of these experiences too is painful. The loss of a part of oneself may be even more difficult than the loss of a loved one. As one grief authority has written, "One loves oneself somehow just a little more than almost anybody else."[1] Life can become rewarding again, with struggle, but it must become so in a different way. A drastic or severe physical change requires a new self-definition: one's self undergoes change.

An ugly marital separation carries certain scars, since all of the lessons are memorized in pain. I have found that I can love and trust another man, but I can never again be deeply in love for the first time, with all the dreams of that young girl who married a man she met during college. There is much happiness in my life now. Still, another love relationship or marriage can never be the same as the first. My innocence is gone.

Losses shatter our virgin thinking. As we lose our innocence, we learn how vulnerable we are. We come to know we are capable of profound suffering. We know we can be hurt in ways previously inconceivable. Afterwards we can never quite forget the fragility of our humanness, no matter how courageously we survive.

Whatever the source of your grief, many who are close to you won't understand what I have just described. When you express feelings of sorrow that "things will never be the same," well-meaning friends and family members will argue with you. They'll try to talk you out of your feelings.

I have heard the most ridiculous comments made to a man whose prostate surgery has left him incontinent, to a woman who has had a breast removed, or to a diabetic who has lost a limb. "Nothing will change, you'll be able to go on," people will say. "Don't grieve over it. Just stay busy." or "Think about all the worse things that could have happened to you!"

We live in a "fix-it" society, in which people think the way to help is to make us feel feelings other than the ones we are actually experiencing. Many persons mistakenly will attempt to offer positive or even cheery words during a time of suffering. What you need instead are friends who can stand alongside you, with patience, while your feelings of sorrow run their course. Feelings cannot be "fixed," as if they were a broken pipe or a leaky faucet. Like a flooded basement, feelings require a lot of work and plenty of fresh air over time to clear the cold dampness away.

Loss has a way of changing our lives dramatically. Even the form of our thoughts about the future undergoes tumultuous alteration. So we ourselves become transformed. Many of the changes will be positive, life-awakening experiences. Some of the transformations will profoundly enrich our lives. However, that is definitely not how life feels to us in the first six months or longer. The idea that learning and personal growth could come from our loss is an almost bothersome idea while we are hurting. It can be annoying when someone else, who is not consumed by our grief, patronizingly suggests it.

Among the rich, deep feelings we must air and speak of openly with people who understand are the memories of the good times, sharing laughter as well as tears.[2] We tend to carry intensified thoughts of these times for quite a long period following a loss. There are many gaps to be filled as we struggle to replace missing experiences or a lost identity. We long for what has been lost — our dream, our loved one, our health, our wholeness. Early in grief we feel angry at having to let go of the person or thing we cherished, and we need to protect ourselves from the awful sense of emptiness that loss entails. In attempting to restore the part of ourselves that has been lost, we tend to glorify the past in order to have the strength to face the future. We remember the best qualities of a person, career, or experience that is now gone from us. Our friends need to understand that we try to cling to happy memories in this way because they are a great comfort to us.

For quite some time, my memory of my husband and the reality of the person he was were two rather different images. But what else could justify the pain? If I held in my mind a broadened sense of the richness of that relationship, it was somehow easier to suffer the loss. I made him in my memory a better man than he probably was because I was hurting and I needed to see the good we shared as more than worth my suffering at the time.

Let's say a man retires or loses his job with a company that has moved overseas. He has an uncomfortable, restless feeling. He hasn't the same identity anymore and has to redefine himself. The same is often true of a woman who has just retired from a job or seen the last of her children leave home. Men and women in this circumstance can't instantly develop a whole new life for themselves, so they may yearn for the past and its comfortable sense of identity until a new self is established. After they have given the prime years of their life to a particular job, it is no wonder that the value of that work needs to be affirmed, even overstated for a time, to justify their years of sacrifice and to be certain that others recognize their accomplishment.

Describing the death of his mother, a high school teacher expressed his feelings: "I was 36 years old and it felt strange to think of a grown man being an orphan, but that's how I felt, having lost both of my parents. Everybody's entitled to a mother, only I don't have one anymore. I don't have something I had yesterday. How will I define myself now?" It is likely that for a time a mother must be remembered as more loving, available, and kind than she was in actual life. The comfort of all that was good helps to make the sense of loss more bearable. Otherwise her loss leaves too great a gap to be filled in the early months. Thinking of oneself in an entirely new way takes time. It is not necessary for you to throw away the good times even though they are sometimes very painful to remember. Your happy memories belong to you and you deserve to keep them. Everybody does. Have the great times and have them fully. But as time goes on, take care that you don't carry your idealization so far that you lose the reality of what you have lost.

Life as it actually is, though imperfect and vastly complicated with sorrow, is richer than life that is idealized. Why do I say so? Because life as it actually is requires of us the courage to depend on the love of other human beings in order to survive. Those whom we love most and who bring us the greatest joy are the persons we've needed to lean on because of our humanness.

I still hate to think about the self-service car wash that now stands on part of the Oklahoma farm where my family's wheat field was, especially during the stressful times. I need those childhood memories of riding my horse, Pumpkin, across that broad green field. Such memories from the past give me strength now. For many years, even the sight of a housing development on the once open land that adjoined the wheat field saddened me. I avoided driving by it and being forced to acknowledge how times have changed the farmlands I loved. It's sweeter to hold the memories of the terraces and the clover.

However, the life of that farm girl never was as glorious in reality as it is in my heart and mind now. The hardships of older days tend to be forgotten. The truth is that an enormous amount of work was involved in growing up on a farm. I believe there is some wisdom in what a lot of people from rural backgrounds will tell you about the character-building virtues of farm life. But as a youngster I wasn't thinking about my character development. I was wondering why my school friends took summer vacations with their parents while we stayed home with the livestock. When I was riding my horse after the milk cow, I was often wishing to be like other, "normal" kids, who had bicycles and could stay and play after school. During periods of difficulty we go back in our minds to earlier times, selecting only the best of the past. Then, at least in our memories, we were more comfortable.

Sudden thunderstorms did come across those open plains where I lived with my family years ago. Both literally and in symbolic ways, vast blue skies could be overrun by the blackness that engulfed us, seemingly from nowhere. I would like to think that I was never hurt as a child as much as I've been hurt as an adult, but that probably was not true. Still, during emotionally difficult periods of my adult life I return to those Oklahoma flatlands for comfort. Then, at least I was a child and didn't have to take care of myself. This attitude characterizes one stage of the grief process, which psychologists call *idealization*. In the words of poet Peter McWilliams, "I am missing you/far better than/I ever loved you."[3]

If I take with me what is real and actual about those early days on the farm, then I can take them with me forever. As long as the two are kept together, no one can rob the red dirt from under me by shattering an illusion that it was all good. Nevertheless, it's okay that at certain times, for the sake of strength, I remember only what was wonderful.

It's all right that sometimes you need to do the same thing.

3. FEELINGS OF GUILT AND SELF-BLAME

It's an awfully risky thing to live.

— Carl Rogers

Seven-year-old Matthew, whose five-year-old brother had died six months earlier, brought home a sentence completion schoolwork assignment. The first five words were the teacher's and the last five words were his. "The worst thing about me," Matthew wrote in the rounded awkward script of a second grader, "is that I make mistakes." It was strange to see a little guy whose head didn't yet quite reach my waist thinking thoughts an adult of any age might have.

"If only I had been wiser, chosen differently, acted differently, had better judgment," we say to ourselves, in the grown-up version of Matthew's words. "If only..." sentences are part of the vocabulary of mourning.

My friend Marie was extraordinarily loyal to her father in the last six months of his battle with cancer. In consultation with the attending physician, she took over the elderly man's nursing care and continually saw to it that he was made as comfortable as possible.

Answering her father's strong wish not to be hospitalized, Marie transformed the study of the California home into an attractive sick room. There she devoted her energies to his physical and emotional needs. While he was still able to walk or sit in a chair, she also saw to it that he spent time every day in the living room and kitchen with the family and outside in the sunshine. Anyone could have recognized how mentally stressed but glad she was to be able to serve her dad in this loving way. He died in her arms shortly after Christmas.

In the privacy of a candle-lit restaurant where we sat, my friend spoke the typical words of a person in the early weeks of grief. Marie thought she should have known when her dad was in his final days. "I should have insisted that his physician explain what Dad's dying would be like," she said with a sadness that turned the red-checkered tablecloth gray. "Then I could have badgered the doctor until he prescribed what was needed to ease Dad's pain."

Should she have gotten a hospice nurse? Should she have talked with her father more about his fear of dying? Couldn't she have made him more comfortable at the end? Had she done the right thing by not taking leave from her work during the earlier months of his illness?

Marie wished she had visited her father oftener when her children were growing up, instead of hating him so much for his alcoholism then. She remembered how they had fished and golfed together when she was young, father and oldest daughter. If only she could have done more, given more, and loved him better, she said.

When a loved one dies, we seldom feel that we've done enough. Even when we've offered extraordinary sacrifices, such as my friend offered her father, we still have the feeling that what we gave was not enough.

It was obvious to me that Marie's faithfulness to her father at the end of his life must have been a great comfort to him, but I didn't say so immediately. Grieving people have difficulty seeing what is obvious to others. For the most part, I simply kept quiet and listened as my friend unfolded one regretful feeling after another. Before she could hear my words of reassurance, she needed to describe in detail all the things she *hadn't* done. Later on in the evening I could remind Marie of the many caring activities she *had* performed for her dad. All of us need comfort when we mourn, but comforting words spoken prematurely go right over our heads.

Unrealistic Guilt

Guilty feelings are almost inevitable in the presence of loss. Whatever the situation, in one way or another we're apt to blame ourselves.

While we may genuinely *feel* blameworthy, usually our self-blaming thoughts are unrealistic; we are overly harsh with ourselves. We stretch our imaginations to believe that we are responsible for anticipating or preventing events, which ordinary mortals could not possibly have prevented. Or twisting human-size mistakes into criminal proportions, we feel guilty as if we had intentionally brought harm to ourselves or to another person, which is rarely the case.

The following are examples of the unrealistic guilt I am talking about:

> If I had stayed home that night, the accident would never have happened.

> I don't know why I could never tell my father I loved him while he was alive. It's too late now and I'm to blame.

> I knew he always drank too much at parties and would fight with me if I asked to drive him home. I should have *made* him let me drive.

> I should never have let my kid brother sign up for the military as a way to get through school. His war injuries have changed everything now and it's my fault.

> Maybe if I weren't so selfish and caught up in my work, our marriage could have lasted.

We were too young then, and I didn't know much about raising children when the first one came. If I had been stricter with my boy, maybe he wouldn't be having all these problems now that he's a man.

My wife always said we should try to save money for a crisis. Somehow I could never do that. Now it's all my fault that we haven't the money we desperately need.

I should have insisted that my mother have a yearly Pap smear; cervical cancer is completely curable when detected early with those Pap smear tests. I knew Mother hadn't had a good physical in years, but I didn't want to nag her. If I had pressured her, I could have saved her life.

If only I had stayed in during the early months of the pregnancy and had avoided crowds, maybe I wouldn't have gotten sick and our baby would not have been born with these problems.

He was awfully depressed and said he had thoughts of killing himself; I should have believed he'd go through with it.

We all could have loved better a host of people close to us: our parents, our children, our love partners, our grandparents, our friends, our brothers and sisters, even ourselves. We feel guilty in a time of loss because we're human beings. We will always be capable of greater wisdom in our minds than in our deeds. We don't have gifts of prophecy and we do have limitations.

Recently a colleague of mine went on a disastrous first date with someone she met through an online dating service. She was shocked to discover that he was nothing like the person he had represented himself to be in a dozen or more written exchanges. In conversation after dinner, he even fantasized about a series of deviant sex acts she found repulsive. My colleague (a sister psychologist) was furious with herself for not seeing ahead of time what a "creep" the man was. Disturbed and disgusted by the experience, the next morning she called me and our mutual friend, Janyne, and asked us to meet her for lunch. Sitting around a dining room table in my home, Janyne (a physician) tried to bring compassion to our colleague as she struggled with self-blame. With all the training she had in human behavior, our psychologist friend kept repeating that she "should have seen this coming." Reaching across the table and taking our colleague's hands in hers, Janyne urged her to be kinder to herself. "You have a doctor's degree in psychology," Janyne said. "Not a doctor's degree in God!"

My own doctor was like a priest to me during times when I felt guilty in a period of mourning. "If you had been able to act differently then, you would have acted differently," she would say. It took me a long time to realize that it is simply not in our power to play out our lives in perfect ways.

Usually guilt feelings need to be answered by another person. The kindest way of helping yourself is to find a friend who will listen attentively to your feelings of self-blame and who will afterwards remind you of all the ways you are not to blame.

One of the resident physicians at the community hospital where I used to teach sought my advice concerning a recently widowed woman with profound feelings of guilt. The woman's husband had died of a heart attack within minutes after they had had sexual intercourse. She blamed herself for her husband's death.

Remembering a supervisor in my training who had once explained to me how to help people separate realistic from unrealistic guilt, I gave the widow's physician a list of questions he should ask her: Why does she feel that *she* is to blame? Does this woman know that having intercourse is not a one-person decision? Did the husband's heart specialist tell them that their normal sexual relations should cease entirely? If they were not medically cautioned, how could she have known what the consequences would be?

"Let's suppose another situation," I said. "Suppose the heart specialist did order the husband to discontinue all sexual relations. Still there are important questions to be asked: Hadn't it been difficult for them not to express their caring for each other in a physical way? Had her husband missed their lovemaking? Had she?"

Many people half-jokingly say that there would be no better way to die than on the tennis court or in bed making love. Whether the husband disobeyed doctor's orders or not, I wondered if the husband might not have been glad to die in the setting of shared intimacy with his wife of forty years. "Ask her," I told the young physician, "if she can accept that idea. Tell her you know that his death is a traumatic event for her and that her grief is very difficult. Then ask if it's meaningful to her that their last moments together were intimate and loving."

If others try to comfort us by arguing too soon with our words of self-blame, we think to ourselves, "If only you knew the whole story, you'd know why I'm to blame." So I advised the widow's physician to let her tell him the full account of her guilty feelings. By listening attentively for signals of unrealism in the events she described, eventually he could help her to recognize how she was blaming herself unnecessarily.

She might say to her physician, "We shouldn't have been having sex. The autopsy showed that he had a severe coronary artery blockage." The widow's physician could then reply, "But how could you have known that? Even the medical people didn't know it until after the autopsy."

A comforting friend will help us to separate realistic from unrealistic guilt by asking questions. Always the crucial questions are

How could you have known that?

Are you expecting yourself to have known things that couldn't have been known with certainty?

Are you tormenting yourself with thoughts of self-blame, as if the other person had no choice or responsibility at all for the events that happened?

As time goes on, we learn from the kindness of others to ask ourselves questions that are similarly kind. Gradually, our feelings of unrealistic guilt begin to diminish.

Realistic Guilt

There isn't another human emotion as excruciatingly painful as the emotion of regret. Sometimes our feelings of regret are absolutely fierce because we are directly responsible for a terrible loss that has come to us or to another person.

If you were driving an automobile that crashed, bringing serious injury or death to someone, you may be tormented with feelings of guilt. If you were driving carelessly, speeding, or driving while intoxicated, your feelings of self-blame probably feel irreconcilable.

If by accident, with a firearm in your hand, you have maimed or killed a loved one or an innocent stranger, feelings of guilt may haunt you day and night.

Perhaps you were away from home for only a brief time when a catastrophic accident, fire, or rape victimized your unattended child. Particularly if the child has suffered permanent harm or death, your sense of sorrowful regret will be overwhelming. You'll desperately need the love of your friends and probably professional help to see you through your months of crisis.

At any time when our own careless behavior brings suffering to another person, it is virtually impossible not to blame ourselves. In fact, people who are psychologically healthy generally do blame themselves in a situation of genuine negligence. Especially when a loved one has been taken from us or been gravely injured by a negligent action of ours, our feelings of remorse are almost unbearably bitter; we may even deny that the event has happened for a period of many months as a way of surviving the assault of guilt we would otherwise feel.

Randy and Richard were identical twins who sometimes visited their aunt and uncle on the rabbit farm that adjoined the wheatland where I was reared. We played cowboys and other summer games together as children. The twins carried a secret between them that is still vivid to me all these years later. I became a keeper of the secret when I asked their aunt one day how Randy came to have a glass eye. She told me never to mention it to the boys because it was a very sensitive subject. Richard had accidentally shot his brother in the eye with a BB gun. "Richard still feels very bad about the accident, so don't speak of it," Mrs. Anderson said. Even at age ten, I recognized the seriousness of the knowledge she was entrusting to me. I never mentioned it again.

Looking back now, I wonder how young Richard dealt with his guilt. Nearly 60 now, has he forgiven himself? No doubt his glass-eyed twin brother forgave him long ago. It is almost always easier to be the victim in such a situation than to be the one whose carelessness brought about the loss.

Whether Richard's guilt has been carried all these years or was left behind in childhood is largely dependent on how the twins' parents handled the tragic event. Did they show concern for Richard's troublesome feelings or was parental concern expressed only for the injured boy?

Probably Richard received a lecture on accidents and carelessness. Perhaps the boys had their gun taken away from them until they were older. The lecture and the terror of the event itself would have been enough punishment. Children, as well as adults, don't need to be harshly lectured after an accident. Usually the lesson has already been learned tenfold. Harsh words only create more problems.

I have no idea how the event that led to Randy's artificial eye came to be regarded in the twins' family. I do know, however, the important questions to be asked: After the initial shock, were angry words spoken to Richard, attacking his character? Calling him names? Accusing him of intentionally bringing harm to his brother? In other words, was he punished with inappropriate severity? Did the parents never let him forget it, always referring to Richard's negligence with the BB gun whenever he caused trouble months and years later? I certainly hope not, for such parental behavior can scar a young person with guilt for a lifetime.

I hope someone in the family made it clear to Richard that accidents can happen to anybody. Wise parents would have seen to it that their continuing love and acceptance of Richard were made obvious to him at the time of the tragedy and thereafter. Despite the seriousness of the permanent loss he accidentally caused his brother, it simply helps no one when guilt is nurtured and allowed to go on and on.

Making peace with ourselves isn't easy, and it takes a long time. When realistic guilt is present, unless loving human beings come along to save us from ourselves, we may become self-destructive in a host of ways in order to punish ourselves for the loss we caused. A child or teenager with unresolved guilt, for example, might become a troublemaker with the unconscious motive of receiving punishment again and again for a wrong action in the past. Children act out their troublesome feelings behaviorally. Following a loss event of any kind, a significant change in behavior that persists for more than several weeks often signals that the child is having difficulty. A normally active child who becomes withdrawn or a normally quiet child who becomes hyperactive may be struggling with guilt.[1]

We are human beings. There is not one of us who has never been negligent. At one time or another, all of us have been careless with our lives or with the life and health of another person. Most of us can't remember our moments of negligence because no disaster happened as a result. Still, accidents and negligence are a part of the human condition.

In a time of sorrow, even when we are faultless or only remotely at fault, we're likely to blame ourselves. A powerful example is the widow in a famous London study who felt guilty for never having made bread pudding for her husband when he was alive.[2] If we feel guilty over such incredibly minor sins of omission, it is no wonder the torment our minds bring us when we are the direct cause of a great loss. The widow's guilt about never making bread pudding is a passing feeling of regret. It is quite another matter when guilt is based on a realistic appraisal of our own behavior. When genuine culpability is involved, our regretful feelings are not transitory; they are fierce and longstanding. Realistic guilt is the sorrowful feeling of an understandably deep and abiding sense of regret.

In a situation of intense remorse, there is not much our friends can say to help us feel less guilty. Usually all that a loving friend or family member can do is make it clear to us that we are loved and accepted despite what has happened. We know from studies of drivers in fatal accidents and others involved in accidentally killing someone that a listening ear and kindness is the most important help anyone can receive or provide.[3]

You'll need understanding friends who can be comfortable with hearing your feelings of regret, spoken again and again. Try to believe that your friends' acceptance and love toward you is genuine. It *is* genuine — because good friends, at least those who are honest with themselves, know that the same or a similar event could have happened to them.

It can also help you to remember that most of us live as best we can, given the persons we are and the state of mind or knowledge we have at a certain point in time. Except in very rare cases involving crimes of passion, mental illness, or acts of violence, people do not intentionally set out to harm others. Neither did you intend the loss event that you're struggling with.

Realistic guilt often requires professional help. If you feel comfortable talking with a minister, priest, or rabbi, such a person is especially competent to help you receive forgiveness in such a situation. A trained counselor, psychologist, or psychiatrist could also help you unburden yourself. Without help you are likely to hold on to your guilty feelings as a way of punishing yourself. A state of depression may engulf you for months or years. You may also begin to engage in a variety of self-destructive behaviors such as excessive drinking and eating, accident proneness, carelessness toward your own health, or self-sabotage in love relationships or at work. It isn't necessary for you to become a tyrant to yourself because an action of yours has brought suffering to another person. You can welcome yourself back to the human race without paying the price of punishing yourself for the rest of your life.

If you believe in a God who accepts and forgives our humanness, that belief will probably help you. With or without this belief, it is important for you to trust in the power of other people who can help you to accept and love yourself.

Moving beyond Guilty Feelings

The most important thing in dealing with guilt is understanding its inevitability, whether realistic or unrealistic. When we can begin to appreciate the normality of our troublesome feelings, we aren't so alarmed by them.

Jack, a former Olympic skier, shared with me the feelings of guilt he had for many years after the death of his baby sister. "I was 12 years old when she died and I remember feeling glad that I wouldn't have to change her diapers anymore. I felt like a bad and terrible person for these thoughts until I was well into my 20s."

Thoughts such as Jack has described are not abnormal or cruel; they're simply one part of the grieving process through which many pass. A noted expert in the area of death and dying, Dr. Elisabeth Kübler-Ross, studied this guilt phenomenon in children after the death of a sibling. Healthy brothers and sisters, she noted, feel jealousy because an ill sibling receives extra parental attention. Sometimes the well children secretly wish the ill child would "go away" so that they might regain their parents' affections and attention. Having thus resented the child who is ill, well brothers and sisters then feel guilty when the ill child dies, as if their wishes had caused the death.[4] Children are highly superstitious and believe an event can be made to happen by one's simply wishing it.

As adults, we often feel a sense of relief when someone dies, particularly if there has been a long illness and we've lived in dread of the final event. Perhaps our loved one was suffering terribly and we wished or prayed for the person to die. After death occurs, we may feel guilty in the same way that children do, thinking our wishes have the power of fulfillment.

Another form of guilt results when certain loved persons die many years ahead of their time and many years ahead of us. In our grief, we cherish them and perceive their integrity and goodness as greater than our own. In the 1970s I counseled many young men returning to college after combat service in Vietnam. I was astonished at how many of these men felt guilty for coming home alive. As one highly decorated soldier put it, "I knew and loved better men than me who died there." Many veterans of the Iraq and Afghanistan wars — especially those who have been deployed repeatedly — report experiencing a similar "survivor's guilt." Such feelings are among the many "invisible wounds of war."[5]

In almost every situation, it is outside the realm of anybody's power to determine which persons live and which die. You need not impose on yourself a penalty for your own life and health or good fortune simply because others suffer terribly. We can live useful lives in appreciation of our own health and continuing existence. No more than that is required of us.

Earlier I mentioned "if only" sentences as part of the vocabulary of mourning. That is certainly true. It is a fact equally central to life's reality, however, that we cannot allow ourselves to live out our lives with "what ifs."

Perhaps the widow's husband I described would have lived another six months or longer if they hadn't made love on that night. However, isn't it also possible that without a normal sex life the husband or the couple could have built up tension, and he could have had a heart attack from the tension?

"What if" you busied yourself with dragging your mother to the doctor for her yearly checkup, took on extra work to save money for a future crisis, and spent the rest of your time reading psychology books which tell young parents how not to ruin their children's lives? In that case, you might never have gotten around to replacing the bald tires on your car and to investing more time in making your marriage work. You might have had a serious automobile accident and a divorce on your hands at the same time. My point, though overstated, is basic: it's not possible to be everywhere at once.

Life requires all of us to make choices. Inescapably we make some wise choices and some foolish ones. And sometimes, in our choosing, we make enormously painful mistakes. In loving certain persons, we cannot avoid neglecting others. In taking care of ourselves reasonably well, carrying out duties at home, school, or work, we cannot find the extra energy for those who need more from us. It's hard to accept these human limitations.

"What ifs" go almost hand in glove with grieving. Most of us need a few weeks or months of rehearsing how things might otherwise have been or how we might have acted differently. Whether your guilt is realistic or unrealistic, the time to move on will come. You will find that you no longer need to blame yourself.

4. PHYSICAL EXPRESSIONS OF LOSS

When you are sorrowful look again in
your heart, and you shall see that in
truth you are weeping for that which
has been your delight.

— Kahlil Gibran

A wide range of marked physical changes can accompany an experience of loss. Not only through tears do we cry out pangs of grief. Under the stress of what has been unrecoverably lost, our bodies have a dozen ways of weeping with us.

Anxiety

One of the people I most respected and admired in my counseling work was Mr. Roland. He was a postal worker in his mid-30s who rarely had any illnesses. On the job one day, Mr. Roland suddenly had sensations of heat in his chest, dizziness, shortness of breath, and shakiness. Since his father had died of a heart attack at age 40, Mr. Roland was terrified. He was certain that he too had heart trouble.

Mr. Roland went into the local hospital for a battery of tests. When the tests showed no medical problems, it was suggested that he talk with me. Sometimes our bodies tell us what our minds can't. Mr. Roland's heart was heavy, but he had no idea of the extent of the emotional pain that was stirring inside of him.

At the hospital I talked with Mr. Roland nearly every day for three weeks. As his story unfolded, Mr. Roland described a younger sister who had been suffering for nine years from an increasingly crippling spinal and brain tumor disease. Although his sister's health had deteriorated dramatically in recent years, Mr. Roland said that he hadn't had to worry about her care because his mother was in good health and able to care for the sister. Now their mother was dying of cancer.

Always there is a keenly important question that a person asks someone in crisis: "When did you last feel well?" In response to this question, Mr. Roland replied that he felt fine six weeks ago, before he and his wife had traveled to Georgia. In Georgia, they visited his ill mother, who had recently become bedridden, and his sister, whose blind and debilitating condition had worsened since Mr. Roland last visited them. During the visit, the family doctor explained to Mr. Roland that his mother's cancer could take her life at any time and that his sister would soon require care in a nursing home. Mr. Roland's insomnia, loss of appetite, heart palpitations, shakiness, and other physical symptoms began shortly after he and his family returned home from Atlanta. Now it made sense why Mr. Roland suddenly became overwhelmed with anxiety, left work that day, and drove in a panic to a nearby hospital. He wasn't having a heart attack, but his heart was troubled.

When he first came for counseling, Mr. Roland had no idea of the extent of his grief over the painful state of affairs of his family. Like his hard-working laborer father, Mr. Roland was not a man to complain or to allow himself emotional expression. "Even when my father died, I shed no tears," he said. He was the oldest child, happily married, a responsible worker, seldom depressed. "People would say of me that nothing ever bothers me," Mr. Roland once told me. "But I'm afraid," he continued, his hands trembling slightly. "That's why I need your help."

Unfortunately, our society continues to place cruel expectations upon men when it comes to the free expression of emotion. From his teenage years onward, Mr. Roland played out a social role that has equated masculinity with keeping one's emotions highly controlled. When it became utterly necessary for this sturdy man to mourn openly, it wasn't easy for him to allow himself the emotions of sorrow, guilt, anger, hopelessness, and fear.

I think I so much liked working with Mr. Roland because of his courage and sensitivity. He entered a delayed mourning process, mourning first his sister's terrible illness, then his father's death and the approaching death of his mother. I was deeply touched on several occasions when he told me how much it helped him finally to be able to cry. Mr. Roland's anxiety symptoms gradually declined in almost direct proportion to his increasingly open expressions of grief. On the day that he decided to return to work at the post office, Mr. Roland told me that he now felt able to handle his mother's approaching death and the responsibility of arranging his sister's continuing care. He would continue to grieve, but the crisis was past. Mr. Roland had made it to the other side of the worst of his pain.

Aches and Pains

You may experience any number of physical discomforts when dealing with a personal crisis. Headaches, digestive disturbances, and aching limbs are the most common complaints that people have expressed to me. Insomnia, irritability, restlessness, moodiness, and loss of appetite or increased appetite are also frequent complaints. Some people engage in frenzied activity. Others lose interest in activity. Muscle tension, fatigue, poor memory, and difficulty concentrating also can accompany grief. Some people have allergic reactions. Some people have acute anxiety attacks characterized by trembling hands, heart palpitations, dizziness, and shortness of breath. Some people have physical symptoms resembling the illness of the one who has died. Many people experience tearfulness. Studies have demonstrated that younger people show more physical symptoms in a process of mourning than older people.[1] Whatever your age, however, you are likely to be troubled by some physical expressions of loss.

One young woman I know ceased having her menstrual periods for over a year during a time of great stress in her marriage. A thorough gynecological examination and fertility tests provided no medical explanation for this condition. In addition, she suffered stomach pain and severe headaches which medical doctors were unable to attribute to a disease of any kind. As this young woman openly began to grieve the end of her marriage, her stomach pain and headaches went away. Amazingly, in the same month that she filed for divorce, her menstrual cycle resumed a normal pattern.

Of course, physical symptoms can be caused by actual medical problems. For this reason, it's always a good idea to consult your physician if your symptoms persist or worry you. A complete physical exam is good preventive medicine and can reassure you that your symptoms are not cause for concern.

Appetite

One of the most pronounced physical changes has to do with appetite. In the early months, many grieving persons suffer a loss of appetite and an accompanying weight loss. From three months onward, increased appetite and excessive weight gain may become problems.[2] In a time of bereavement, people are more susceptible to physical and emotional illness of many kinds. In the process of your grieving, if you have lost or gained five percent or more of your normal body weight, you should consult your physician.[3]

Whether your interest in eating has significantly diminished or significantly increased, you may be suffering from nutritional deficiency, not uncommon in people under stress who have poor eating habits. Your appetite should gradually stabilize, but it may not do so entirely until more than a year has passed. In the meantime, it is important to remember that foods of high nutritional value will help you to feel better. Emotional stress can be intensified by inadequate or improper nourishment.

If you live alone or do the cooking, you probably don't feel like putting much time into meal preparations. Since many prepackaged foods that are easily prepared are notoriously poor in nutritional value, you would do better to eat seafood, meats, fruits, dairy products, and vegetables that require little preparation. When you lack the energy for cooking, you might also have a good meal at a restaurant or invite yourself to eat with close friends and family members.

Sleep

Grieving people have described to me three kinds of sleep disturbances: the tendencies to awaken early in the morning, to have difficulty falling asleep, and to awaken during the night. You may experience one or more of these sleep difficulties or none at all.

Insomnia is especially a problem in the first few weeks and may continue for some time.[4] You can use a number of strategies to deal with it. Getting physical exercise and talking about your grieving feelings during the day with someone who understands usually are the two best medicines for rest at night. Writing in a journal or typing a long e-mail to a friend who can respond to you later may enable you to go back to bed feeling less burdened.

When we're hurting, various troublesome thoughts swim around in our heads like too many goldfish in a small bowl. Sharing your feelings of grief with a friend, counselor, or clergyperson frees up the space in your brain for some happier thoughts. Getting a massage or taking a yoga class or college course during the day and meditation or prayer are additional sleep aides. Some people find that it helps them to read at night, to lie for a while in a warm bath, or to listen to music. Reading books like this one can help you put that goldfish into a larger aquarium, too.

Taking over-the-counter or prescription medicines for sleep, in my opinion, may be a temporary remedy, but they can cause their own problems beyond a few days or weeks. If your sleep disturbance persists and interferes with your daily functioning, you may be suffering from a severe depression. Your doctor might decide to prescribe an antidepressant. Antidepressants are not addictive and can effectively treat both the sleep problem and the depression.

If you live alone, periodically having a friend or family member stay overnight at your place, as well as occasionally staying overnight with them, can be helpful. Unless you have an alcohol problem, there is nothing wrong with occasionally using alcohol as a way of helping yourself fall asleep. However, you should be very careful never to combine alcohol with any kind of sleeping medication or other medication, and you should be careful not to make a habit of drinking as a way of anesthetizing yourself. Endeavoring to dull your senses on a regular basis will only prolong what is already a complex and time-consuming grieving process. Sleep in humans follows a normal pattern of 90-minute cycles throughout the night; such patterns are interrupted by alcohol, and this is another reason why drinking to fall asleep can cause many more problems than it solves.

Certain kinds of losses cause the nights to be especially lonely. You lie awake feeling empty or preoccupied with memories that have become painful. Perhaps you feel anxious about your future. As psychologist Rollo May has written, the fear of *feeling* our loneliness is more treacherous than the loneliness itself. May tells the story of a man who was terrorized by his fear of being alone. Finally the man ceased his frenzied activity and stood still long enough fully to feel his pain. What he discovered was that his loneliness did not engulf and overpower him in the way that his fear of it had.[5]

Constantly busying yourself in the daytime and fleeing from your feelings of sorrow may only compound your uneasy emotional state at night. That is why I say the best medicine for insomnia is talking specifically about your loss with understanding friends. Talking in a generalized, emotion-detached manner usually doesn't help, but sharing your specific troublesome feelings and organizing your thoughts does bring relief, in little doses, over a period of time.

Through every crisis of my adult life, I've been blessed with friends comfortable with tears and with strong feelings. Through phone calls, e-mail, letters, and visits, your friends also can be a great help to you, but you'll have to reach out to them.

Grieving people have a strong tendency to withdraw from human contact. At the time that we are most in need of the company of other people, we tend to avoid activities and relationships that we once pursued with interest. One researcher found that the widows he followed in a 13-month study spent four-fifths of their time at home, often isolating themselves from friends and family.[6] A strong act of will may be required on your part to reverse this powerful inclination to withdraw from others in your time of mourning.

In graduate school I was involved in a process of grieving that was being helped along by a hospital chaplain. Sometimes in these therapy sessions I would cry to the point where my face showed it afterwards, and I would rush to the ladies' room at the end of the session to reconstruct my hair and makeup. In this way I could look presentable to the staff and patients when I rode the elevator back to my responsibilities in the medical ward.

One day when this sequence of events was in progress, I came out of the washroom after about ten minutes and saw the broad-shouldered back of the chaplain as he walked down the hospital corridor, away from his office and around a corner, whistling. I thought to myself, "I've just spent an hour with this guy, crying so much that my face looks a wreck; and here *he* is now, walking off in a bouncing gait, whistling a happy tune!" I was furious with him.

I didn't understand the chaplain's behavior then. I understand it now. Recently a nurse assigned to an intensive care unit asked me during a hospital course I was teaching how I manage to work daily with grieving people "without going around with a long face." I told the nurse and her colleagues the story of the whistling chaplain. "He had good reason to be in a happy mood," I said. "I was hurting and expressing the hurt — but it was what I needed to do to feel better."

Often I feel in a positive mood when someone leaves my office after crying. This is in no way a depreciation of the person's dignity or pain. My mood simply reflects the knowledge that the process of healing is underway. As the weeping person departs, I think to myself or say aloud to him or her, "Well, you'll probably be able to sleep tonight."

If your friends seem alarmed by your many troublesome emotions, you may have to explain that you're not "falling apart," that you don't need advice, that your feelings are very painful but normal, and that you already feel better having talked about them. When friends understand the process you're going through, they will know that they are helping you by listening and sharing your pain. Then everybody can have an easier time going to sleep.

Even with good friends and the ability to continue to work, some physical expressions of loss may be a discomfort to you early in grief and on a periodic basis thereafter. You can be reassured by the knowledge that for many people physical symptoms are simply a part of the normal grieving process. We yearn to recover what has been lost and our bodies cry out that yearning.

5. ANGER AND BITTERNESS CAN BE A GOOD SIGN

Anger is an energy. It cannot be destroyed or forgotten. It has to be converted.

— Leo Madow

Anger

While studying at Duke University, I was working as a chaplain intern in North Carolina, counseling young people in crisis. I was still pretty inexperienced when it came to knowing how to recognize dangerous situations in advance of a catastrophe.

Eighteen-year-old Brian walked through my door for his first counseling session with his arm curled around a motorcycle helmet. He looked a little like an overly thin high school football player coming into the locker room after taking a beating on the field. We talked for nearly two hours, but I was unable to get any part of the story of his battered spirits out of him. That was on Wednesday.

Thursday night I was called to the hospital emergency room by Brian's parents. In an apparent period of depression, Brian had shot himself in the abdomen with a shotgun. His action could have been a genuine accident, but it probably wasn't.

By the time I drove across town, he was in surgery. I met his parents in the waiting area outside the operating room. The place was much too quiet. We sat in a row on a bench with soft padding, Brian's father and I on either side of his mother. I thought I had come to console them, but their parental reaction wasn't what I expected. While it was still uncertain whether the young man would live or die, his mother repeated several times an angry statement that at the time was startling to me. "He has always caused trouble, and now he has done it again! How can he do this to us?" She began angrily to recite every worry Brian had given them in 18 years. Meanwhile, Brian's father brought forth no argument to his wife's anger. He simply sat with his eyes blankly fixed on the sterile white wall in front of us.

I remember feeling rather judgmental and superior to these bewildered parents. "Dear God," I thought to myself, "their only son may be dying on the operating table and they're angry at him!" I was unaware then of the normalcy of such feelings of fury.

Staring at Brian's chest to monitor his breathing, I sat all night in his hospital room thinking. Every time the nurse came in to check his pulse and blood pressure, a little anger grew in me at the thought that he might not give me a chance to help him. Maybe his parents weren't so strange for feeling angry. As grieving people often do at the beginning, I was more absorbed in reviewing our conversation of the day before, wondering if I was to blame in some way.

He came through it all after a very ugly period of recuperation and has now made quite a good life for himself, his wife, and his children. But I learned some things from that event that I won't ever forget. Brian's first cognizant words to me were, "When cowboys are shot on the movie screen, it's not gory and painful like this."

Whenever life puts us up against a wall, for whatever reason, great anger is usually generated within us. Some people, like Brian's parents, are immediately angry in the face of loss. Their feelings focus quickly on the most obvious cause of their anger. Others are more apt to express a generalized fury, the buckshot effect of a wide array of angry feelings expressed toward work associates, relatives, friends, and the like. Still others are preoccupied with worrisome emotions in the early months of grief, unaware of the angry feelings held tightly within themselves.

Sometimes our anger is combined with envy. A neighbor of mine was furious that his beloved stepmother died before he could drive the distance from Baltimore to Pennsylvania, where she had been suddenly hospitalized. He felt envious of the other family members who were able to see her before she died. He was in such a rage over not having been called sooner that a physician tried to medicate him at the hospital. "How could she die without waiting for me to get here?" he shouted. "The others got to see her!"

Childhood

Many of us grew up in an atmosphere where angry feelings were unacceptable to the adults who provided for us and taught us. For us, there was to be no talking back, no raising our voices, no door slamming or foot stomping. So we closed the door gently 14 consecutive times or descended and ascended the stairway softly twice in a row. Possibly you were put to bed when you were angry or you were forced to apologize politely to your kid brother when you felt like punching him in the mouth. Some of us, as angry youngsters, heard words such as "get that ugly look off your face!" We weren't supposed to show, even by our facial expressions, whatever frustration or fury we were feeling inside. By the time one of these family scenarios was over, we were angrier than ever.

What I have described is not exactly the kind of upbringing that teaches a young person to explore and understand feelings of anger. Especially when we're grown and a crisis comes, we need desperately to know how to do that.

A physician at a hospital where I used to teach once told me that in his opinion all anger is an indication of immaturity. I thought to myself that that's probably what he had been told as an angry but normal youngster when a best friend broke his confidence, a new bicycle fell apart without any help from him, or his parents embarrassed him in public. If we are taught early to think of anger as a "childish feeling," it's not easy for us to unlearn this attitude.

In my religious upbringing I was instructed to think "nice thoughts." As a child I believed that holding anger in one's heart was as wrong as committing an act of violence against another person. Even as an adult I was persuaded that a "good person" did not think angry thoughts, much less express them. Finally, after a year or more of psychotherapy, I found a place in my mind for the realization that my thoughts don't hurt anybody. "Your fantasies are free," my doctor once said to me, "but you impose a penalty."

Possibly your early experience was not as I have described. Instead of being raised in a home where anger was denied, shamed, or punished, perhaps you frequently witnessed an anger of the kind that is explosive and destructive. Such might have been the case, for example, in a home with an alcoholic or abusive parent. In this event you are apt to have determined at a very young age that all anger is hurtful, frightening, or destructive. You may have vowed to yourself never to unbottle strong emotion in the way that it was poured upon the victims in your family. Today you may be fearful even of benign anger because you've seen anger so destructively expressed. Following the parent model you witnessed, it is also possible that you "caught" the personality trait of an explosive temper. When parents have trouble controlling their negative emotions, children grow up to have problems with anger and hostility as well.[1]

It all comes down to a common ground. As the authors of the book *Creative Aggression* have described, many people for most of their lives have associated feelings of anger with disastrous consequences: abandonment, excessive punishment, doom-oriented threats, destruction, even threats of dying.[2] The "anger equals disaster" equation may have been learned in your family. It may also have been learned from religious teachings that God condemns and punishes human feelings rather than understands and forgives them. These teachings can do a lot of damage.

Human beings are amazing creatures, capable of an incredible variety of adaptive behaviors. Having learned as children that certain feelings were unacceptable to those whose approval and love we sought, we convinced ourselves that such feelings do not exist within us. When stricken by a crisis as adults, then, we have difficulty being aware of even strong angry feelings buried inside ourselves, feelings that cry out for expression as a part of the healing process.

Reverend Baker was 55 years old. For 30 years he had been the devoted servant of his parishioners, the kind of man who always put his own needs last. Had you asked a member of his Episcopal congregation to describe Reverend Baker's personality, you would have heard that he was "rarely angry," "almost always easygoing," and "the kind of man who quietly accepts whatever comes his way." Yet Reverend Baker was plagued by an advanced case of ulcerative colitis, a painful condition.

As we reviewed the history of his 12-year illness, which had grown progressively worse, Reverend Baker repeatedly told me, "I'm not angry. It's just one of those things." Our discussions began to center around the medically acknowledged role that stress plays in exacerbating colitis. Gradually his angry feelings surfaced. He finally acknowledged his anger at parishioners who phoned him late at night over inconsequential matters. "If somebody is really in trouble, that's different," he said. "But my people call me on my day off, when I'm with my family on a holiday, and in the middle of the night — to ask about things that have nothing to do with a crisis." Also, an issue that engendered resentment, he said, was the fact that many parishioners ignored his dietary restrictions when inviting him to dinner. Reverend Baker seemed surprised to be discovering within himself these feelings of anger. "I never realized before that I was bothered by all of this," he said. As time went on, Reverend Baker also became aware that he was angry at the illness itself. "This illness is so embarrassing," he protested, recalling his bouts with the diarrhea that is part of the condition. "Why couldn't I have had some other illness?" Ventilating the anger seemed to help him. He began to set realistic limits with his parishioners. And, having protested, Reverend Baker could live more comfortably with his medical condition.

Interrupted Life

No matter how much we wish it weren't so, anger is unavoidable in life, particularly in the face of loss. One of the few times anger isn't an important aspect of the grieving process is when an elderly loved one dies after having lived a full and happy life. Sometimes our grief on such an occasion is free of regret and emotional turmoil. We may be sad and miss our loved one, but unless the person was our marriage partner or one we were otherwise greatly dependent on, it's the kind of loss that seems to us just and fair.

We also feel angry when an untimely crisis interrupts our living and dreaming. One young woman doctor I know became pregnant while faithfully using birth control. "With a 97 percent chance of not getting pregnant," she exclaimed, "why should *I* be one of the women for whom the contraceptive didn't work?" As commonly happens, Dr. Carr's anger at having to choose her residency over her pregnancy spun off in other directions. "If more women were doctors and scientists," she raged, "we'd have reliable contraceptives for men! Why do *women* have to take all the risks?"

Most of us ask "Why me?" when we suffer loss. The fact is that there is no fairness in war, disease, natural disasters, accidents, divorce, birth defects, rape, or death. People who live recklessly can suffer terribly, and so can those of us who try to take good care of ourselves.

Protest

Suffering the loss of someone or something precious commonly produces a sense of protest. This is true whether the loss was beyond our control or was in some way chosen. Normally, it is not so important *when* our feelings of protest find the light of day. What matters is that at some point we recognize and express our feelings of bitterness. We may not be consciously aware of these feelings, but usually the anger is present and will take its toll in hidden ways if not brought out into the open.

A wide variety of symptoms can signal the presence of hidden anger: depression, accident proneness, irritability, erratic sleep patterns, fatigue, excessive drinking or overeating, headaches, backaches, and many other physical complaints. Unresolved anger can lead to illness, a need to fail, or a need to sabotage our own happiness. Hidden anger can even be the source of suicidal feelings and high-risk behavior that can endanger oneself and others.

Theresa, the young woman in Chapter 1 whose brother committed suicide, had a very difficult time bringing to the surface her feelings of anger toward her brother. Generally it is true that anger toward the one who died, became sick, or was injured in an accident is the most difficult anger to allow ourselves to feel. Because we feel guilty when angry in such situations, we frequently disguise our anger toward the one we lost, expressing our fury only indirectly.

I first realized that Theresa was feeling angry at her brother when she came one night for her counseling session angry at people who smoke cigarettes. These days it is hard to believe there was ever a time when therapists smoked with their clients, but that's how it was when I was a young counselor and still a smoker. A college student, Theresa launched a tirade about her classrooms where, also at that time, professors were allowing people to smoke. "I'd like to spray insecticide all over the classroom and have everybody breathe it," she said, "like I have to breathe *your* smoke!"

Not having a completely thick head, I immediately put out my lighted cigarette! After telling Theresa that I would never again smoke during her counseling sessions, I focused on the meaning of her anger. "I guess you feel pretty angry at people whose self-destructiveness brings you suffering," I said.

It was still too soon in her grieving process for Theresa to let herself feel angry at her brother. She was simply *outraged*, she told me, at self-destructive people in general, smokers in particular, and the harm such persons bring to others. It was another three months before Theresa was able to say, without feeling terribly guilty, how furious at her brother she was that he chose to commit suicide rather than seek help.

Anger is a struggle with holding on and letting go and it is a struggle with evil. We feel angry at the unfairness of life that we should have to suffer the loss we are facing. We feel angry at those who do not understand our pain and who appear to be so secure, safe, and distant from knowing personally what our suffering is all about. We feel angry at whoever or whatever is the cause of our loss, angry at the one who dies for abandoning us. Not uncommonly, we feel angry at life in general. We search around for someone to blame.

In the words of pastoral counselor Dorothy Yoder Nyce, "Whether recognized as such or not, the basic questions are often directed toward God: 'Why must we suffer? Does suffering have meaning? What is there for me to learn from suffering?' "[3] As Rabbi Kushner has written in the bestseller, *When Bad Things Happen to Good People*, "Because we were brought up to believe that everything that happens is His [God's] will, we hold Him responsible for what happened, or at the very least for not having prevented it from happening."[4]

Suffering in human life does not come to people in equal or rational proportions. If it did, we might be able to accept it more readily. When friends say, "Don't be bitter" or "Don't blame God," they simply don't understand. If we could order our troublesome feelings away, most of us would be happy to do that. But, generally, we can't help feeling angry, and frequently this anger includes feeling furious at God.

In the grieving process, feeling angry is often a positive indication that gradually we are facing and accepting a hurtful separation. Depression, preoccupation, idealization, guilt, and self-blame are deeply inward experiences, equally necessary to the process of mourning. However, when we begin to feel resentful or angry, that feeling can be a sign that we are mobilizing our energies again and fighting. Our emotions are turning outward.

Dealing with Anger

You don't have to feel ashamed of bitter feelings. You can remind yourself and your friends that your feelings of protest will not last forever but that feeling angry for a time is necessary and helpful.

Louise, whose spiritual crisis was described in Chapter 2, was angry at God that all her efforts to be good did not protect her from suffering. In my office that night I asked Louise to take her hands down from her face and to carry on a conversation with God out loud, in my presence. "Tell God how angry you are with Him," I said. "Tell Him that this suffering you are facing is not your idea of being rewarded for your faithfulness."

Although hesitant at first, Louise was able to talk to an empty chair, pretending God was in the chair and explaining her feelings of anger. "This just isn't *fair*," she said. "I've been loyal to You for 47 years!" Her voice grew louder and louder. "We've raised every child in the church and I gave everything I had to those children and to my husband! How can we be having all these problems now? I tried everything I knew to keep our family together!"

I asked Louise to move over to the empty chair and to pretend that she was God, answering Louise. When she was sitting in the other chair, I said, cooperating with the fantasy, "God, Louise is very upset. She has been crying for 30 minutes now, and she's furious at You. What have You to say to her?"

God, not having the problem with words that mortals do, in this fantasy had an ability to sum up everything in a single, powerful sentence. "Louise," God said, "I want you to seize your freedom!"

I was deeply touched by these words. I had hoped that somewhere in this woman's experience she had learned of an accepting God who would not condemn her now. I asked her to return to her own chair and to answer what God had just spoken.

"I know, God," she said. "I've never been able to speak any of my feelings before, especially feelings that I thought weren't nice. I know You're telling me that You can accept my anger. That You want me to be free from all these guilty feelings I have, that You never expected me not to complain in 25 years of marriage, that maybe I'd have been better off if years ago I had complained."

After the counseling session, when Louise and I were walking together toward the parking lot, we both started to walk across the grass instead of following the sidewalk. Abruptly, Louise jumped back onto the concrete path, saying, "Oh! I mustn't walk on the grass!"

"No, Louise," I said. "Let's walk on the grass!" She looked my way and caught the symbolic meaning of what I was saying. "You don't have to live so absolutely straight and narrow to be a faithful servant," my eyes said wordlessly. Louise began spontaneously and joyfully to run around in circles, like a young child. "I don't always have to walk on the sidewalk," she exclaimed. "I can run on the grass!"

That was a powerful experience for me. I remember thinking as I drove home that night that whatever else the reality of God is about, it certainly is about receiving acceptance and seizing our freedom.

It is important for most of us that, like Louise, we find expression for our feelings of anger. Such feelings often grow more troublesome the longer they remain hidden. Talking with understanding friends can help a great deal. You may have to search your mind to identify friends, neighbors, or relatives who are able to accept your feelings of anger. Usually such persons are available to you. Talking with others who have experienced anger in a time of loss can help you to feel less unsettled.

Many people are afraid that what has happened to us might happen to them. They are uncomfortable with hearing about our loss and particularly our anger. When a woman has had breast surgery and chemotherapy, she may feel a great sense of unfairness for having had to pay a price for life that most other women aren't required to pay. She may feel that her husband or the man in her life doesn't or can't understand her feelings. She is also likely to find that many women are so afraid of breast cancer themselves that they can't allow her the space she needs to talk of her feelings of sorrow and anger. Her best comfort will probably come from an understanding woman friend, from other women who have suffered the same experience, or from a woman physician or therapist.

Thousands of men who grieve about relinquishing their children in divorce court can find strength and support among other divorced men who share this experience. Not uncommonly, these fathers feel enormous anger at the continuing tendency of courts to rule in favor of the mother.

Groups for ileostomy, colostomy, and mastectomy patients, divorced parents, suicide survivors, people with traumatic brain injuries or cancer, battered women, widows and widowers, infertile couples, bereaved parents, and many others have been established around the country. There are also groups for family members struggling with a loved one's substance abuse, mental illness, or dementia. Where you live, there is probably a support group for people suffering your particular loss, especially if you live in a metropolitan area. Your physician's office, church or synagogue, or community health center may be able to inform you of the existence of such a group.

Group therapy with a psychologist, social worker, or other mental health counselor usually costs a good deal less than does individual therapy. If no other supportive groups exist and you are having difficulty finding understanding people with whom to share your mourning period, group therapy might be helpful to you. A telephone call to a community mental health center might lead you to such a group. Strength can be found in community with others.

Sometimes writing out your anger on paper can be helpful. I often asked persons in counseling with me to write angry letters and read them aloud. It is almost always best never to mail them. Remember that your *thoughts* aren't harmful to anyone and neither are your words shared in private. Many family doctors and clergy are able to be understanding and accepting of anger as a normal reaction to loss. A professional who is comfortable with anger will not cause you to feel shame, guilt, or embarrassment over your feelings.

Some therapists, trained in the Gestalt school, have their patients beat on pillows as a way of releasing anger. This can go on not just a few minutes, but until the person is exhausted or has exhausted the anger within.

Anger can be masked in the form of fear. In our body chemistry, anger and fear are very similar chemical mechanisms. Sometimes, when we believe ourselves to be engulfed in a state of fear, we are actually fighting submerged anger.

By the time I decided to go to divorce court, 18 months after my marital separation, I had already done most of the related grief work. Yet, about a week before I was to appear before the judge to obtain my divorce, I had a strange experience. I began to have a terrible fear of being attacked on the street at night. Once inside the house, I looked behind doors, under the bed, and behind the shower curtain, fearful that someone was hiding there to hurt me. I had never been terrorized by such fears before. Obviously, something was troubling me.

A friend with whom I had worked in Washington, DC, seemed the right person to call for help. I met with Lewis and his wife Ina in their Washington home and described my baffling behavior to them. Lewis, a counselor trained in Gestalt techniques, put pillows on the floor. He wanted me to beat on the pillows and release my anger. "But Lewis," I argued, "I'm not feeling angry. I'm feeling afraid!"

"Never mind," he said, "just try it." And he explained that I should shout, "I'm angry! I'm angry!" over and over again, beating on the pillows. He said I'd soon know what I was angry about. The expression on my face must have shown my embarrassment. I was not crazy about the idea of behaving like a wild person in the presence of another counselor and his wife.

"It's okay," Lewis said, reading my mind. "I went through this when *my* divorce was about to take place."

I doubled my fists and beat on the pillows with all my strength. It was astonishing to me how rapidly "I'm angry! I'm angry!" turned into a furious conversation with the man I was about to divorce. I battered the pillows until my arms ached, yelling at my husband how enraged I was to be stuck with the car payments, most of the cost of the divorce, and all the responsibilities we once shared. My pillow beating went on for 20 minutes or so until, exhausted, I collapsed into tears.

It was several days later before I realized that I hadn't looked behind a door or shower curtain since that afternoon with Lewis and Ina. The fear had gone when the anger was dispersed.

If you decide that you would be helped by an action such as pillow beating, you should remember that you are simply releasing normal human feelings. Of course, pillow beating should be done only in complete privacy or in the company of a therapist or an understanding friend, so that no one will misunderstand your pounding and talking out your anger in fantasy. Nor should you try it unless you are in good physical health and have no high blood pressure or heart problem. If you use this method for ventilating anger, you should never pretend that you are beating on yourself, regardless of whether you think it is yourself that you are angry with. People never come to feel better by hurting themselves or others. Many are likely to cry during the time of the pillow beating or afterwards. Usually it's all just a part of the release of emotion and nothing to be frightened of. If it is too upsetting for you to express your angry feelings in this way, you can stop at any time. There are plenty of other good and healing ways of dealing with such feelings.

As long as a person doesn't get stuck there, the angry phase of grieving frequently is an indication that our healing process is well underway. It signals the fact that we are not denying our loss but facing it. Grieving persons who have been depressed for many weeks or months often begin to feel much better once their angry feelings begin to be resolved.

It is important to remember that the purpose of expressing your anger is to *get beyond it*. Remaining angry will only prevent you from healing and going forward with your life. If you ever want to be happy again, you have to learn to let it go.

6. WHAT ONE GETS IS WHAT ONE RESISTS

It is important to the healing process that you be with the pain, experience the desolation, feel the hurt. Don't deny it or cover it or run away from it. Be with it. Hurt for a while.
— Colgrove, Bloomfield, and McWilliams
How to Survive the Loss of a Love

That people put up a resistance to feelings and thoughts associated with grief is understandable. Grief is a painful process.

The more fully a person works through the emotions and issues that have to be dealt with, the more relief the person will feel. It still isn't easy. Almost without exception, when I've given a public lecture on grief, someone in the audience has asked, "Isn't there any way to make the process less painful?" Or, "Why can't there be a quicker way to recover than having to grieve like this?" I always reply that I wish there was another way.

Mourning remains a process we must all go through. It simply isn't possible to go around it without jeopardizing recovery and healing.

Hurtful, angry, or guilty feelings that we try to deny stay with us for years and years. If we resist what we feel, we continue to have our troublesome feelings and we have them for years. It is better to learn how to *be* our feelings, to surrender to them at times with trusted friends and family or others in whom we confide. When we have gained clarity on our grieving process with all its phases, we often find ourselves freer of conflict and sorrow than we otherwise could ever be.

To a person who seeks my help in finding a good counselor, I'll often explain, in a very few words, my understanding of how people heal. "Usually," I'll say, "healing involves being willing to hurt more for a while in order to hurt much less for the rest of your life." The same is true of sharing grief with understanding friends and family members. Healing is the process of *going through* your troublesome memories, feelings, and conflicts. In the words of Dr. Erich Lindemann, who was a pioneer in studying patterns of grieving, healing is called "grief work" because work is what it is.[1]

Delayed Mourning

When Aaron's mother became gravely ill, Aaron was called home from military service overseas and was able to spend several days with her at the hospital before she died. The Army granted a family emergency leave of one month. This was not enough time, of course, for a son to grieve his mother's sudden illness and death. Aaron's mourning was forced to a halt when he was flown back to his assignment as a combat officer. Once again preoccupied with matters pertaining to his own survival and that of his men, Aaron found himself resisting all feelings of loss.

Three months after his mother's death, a message came through the Red Cross that Aaron's grandfather had died. Because of his responsibilities as an officer, he was refused permission to go home for the funeral. Aaron dearly loved his grandfather and was furious with the Army for denying his request. A mental state of apathy set in. Aaron wasn't feeling much of anything. He began a downward spiral.

Feeling that sorrowful feelings would otherwise overcome him, Aaron rarely spoke of his mother and grandfather in conversations with others. His mother's death was the hardest. Sometimes at night, he pretended that she was still alive, and he almost had himself believing it.

The fact that Aaron was so far away from home made it easier in one sense. Not surrounded by daily reminders, it was easier to carry out the unconscious decision that he made to resist grieving. It was as if a little man with a broom lived in his head 24 hours a day, keeping house and sweeping away any unsettling, hurtful thoughts. The loss of mother and grandfather seemed unreal, and the housekeeper in his head wanted to keep it that way. Even during the time that Aaron was stationed in California after his deployment ended, the full reality of his loss remained continents away.

He was 28 years old when he left the service and entered a middle management position in business. Although two years had passed since his mother died, Aaron still hadn't allowed himself to face the full reality of her death. He had been able to cry on the morning she died, but not a single time since.

With Aaron living again in the house where he was reared, he and his father seemed to argue constantly over trivial things. Their conflicts were a puzzlement to both father and son because they had always gotten along well. On meeting the woman that his father was intending to marry, Aaron found that he intensely disliked everything about her. He resented her and felt guilty for resenting her. When she came to visit, he was infuriated by the sight of her in the house, rearranging things. He could hardly stop from yelling at her to "get the hell out of my mother's kitchen."

Grief doesn't go away just because it is ignored, resisted, or denied. Resisting the loss and one's feelings about it only sends these feelings underground. They can then surface unexpectedly at any time. Aaron still didn't know that it was his unresolved grief that was making him uncomfortable. He felt restless, moody, and unhappy and was abusing alcohol at every opportunity. But he didn't know why.

Supposedly to talk about a drinking problem, he arranged for counseling. Yet in the first hour, his talk turned to family problems. The whole situation seemed to hit him hard, all at once. His mother was dead. Reminders of her were everywhere. With his father in love with "another woman," no longer could he resist the powerful reality of her absence. He began to mourn.

Aaron said that he felt ashamed of himself, a grown man, angry at his father in this way. I pointed out that it was understandable for a son to feel resentful upon returning home to find his dad ready to remarry. After all, in his feelings, his mother had been dead for only 21 days. He had stopped grieving on the day that he boarded a military plane to return to fighting a war.

When he was finally released, Aaron's grief took the normal course. He mourned as one would mourn from the second month onward. Feelings he had resisted earlier he at last expressed. He moved from preoccupation with the loss to depression and weeping. He dealt with his feelings of guilt and self-blame, his pangs of longing, anger, and bitterness.

Aaron told me that despite his best efforts not to think of his mother's death, a single recurring thought had haunted him these many months. He had resisted grieving, burying himself in the responsibilities of a military officer. Still, the thought wouldn't go away: he was to blame for his mother's death.

He remembered the doctor standing in the hospital corridor talking with his father after the autopsy. "She died from a brain tumor," the doctor had said. "The tumor may have been present for many years or it could have been there for only a few months." From that moment, Aaron was plagued by the thought that a head injury years ago had caused his mother's brain tumor.

He was eight years old, the kind of boy whose toys were sometimes strewn everywhere. One day his mother came out of the front door and onto the porch in a hurry, her arms filled with clean laundry to fold. She slipped on a bow-and-arrow set he had left on the floor and fell backwards, hitting her head on the concrete. Aaron convinced himself that the fall must have been what gave her the brain tumor. He had resisted the thought for nearly two years, but it wouldn't go away.

As time went on, it became obvious to me that Aaron's feelings of guilt and self-blame had little to do with the bow and arrow. When the overall process of grief is resisted or denied, a person is apt to get stuck in one stage of grieving and to repeat the stage over and over again. This must be what was happening with Aaron, I decided.

For two years Aaron had resisted the wider range of feelings associated with his loss. The price for that resistance was the recurrent thought of self-blame. When a great dike is built against the onrush of a whole group of feelings, somewhere those feelings will overflow or will back up and flood the lower lands. It isn't possible to shut down the grieving process without having to contend with problematic consequences.

In the process of our talks together, Aaron finally came to examine his "guilt." His mother was not knocked unconscious and showed no vision or memory impairment at the time of her fall or for years after. It was virtually impossible that her brain tumor resulted from that incident. Whatever the circumstances, Aaron's being the normal kind of boy who left his toys around didn't cause his mother's death.

Aaron's guilt feelings were as old as he was. An only child, he had always felt undeserving of the absolute acceptance and approval he received from his parents. He knew that he wasn't entirely the "good boy" they seemed to think he was. As a youngster, Aaron frequently compared himself with other children. "I always felt that I didn't deserve all the extra love and the other things my parents gave me," he said. Aaron remembered being a very small boy, at home with a babysitter, waiting for his parents to return. What seemed like hours passed as he stood in his pajamas looking out his bedroom window after the babysitter thought he was asleep. "I used to be afraid they'd die and never come back," Aaron told me, reliving the feeling. "I guess it was because I felt I didn't deserve them."

I told Aaron that I thought he had finally come upon the reason that he blamed himself for his mother's death. "Your guilt began," I said, "long before she fell over the bow-and-arrow set and your father scolded you for it." For as long as he could remember, Aaron feared that he would lose his mother and that it would be his fault for not deserving her. It is typical childlike thinking to have an exaggerated sense of our own power over others' lives. As grownups, we get into trouble if we continue to think in the same childlike way.

Freud, the founder of modern psychology, emphasized the powerful influence that childhood plays during the crises of our adult lives. Old unresolved issues from childhood have a way of returning. Under stress, in search of a means to cope, we fall back on childhood interpretations. Yearnings and fears that were never put to rest in our earlier days come back to haunt us.

In my experience, regardless of how old or how psychologically healthy we become, we return to childlike ways of seeing things when stricken by hurtful times. It is no wonder, then, that we put up such a fight not to feel our adult losses fully. Feeling the pain, anger, and guilt often sends us back into remembering and feeling childhood pain, anger, and guilt. For many people, this is a necessary part of the healing process.

Years later, as I was writing this book, I made it a point to contact Aaron. It had been a long time since we last talked. I asked him if he was ever troubled again by self-blaming thoughts concerning the loss of his mother. "No," he said, "after I saw why I interpreted things that way, I quit feeling guilty." Aaron had been fully able to mourn the loss of his mother and grandfather. In the months and years that followed, he accepted his father's remarriage and actually became quite fond of his stepmother.

Water, as it freezes and the molecules expand, has the power to burst steel pipes wide open. Likewise, frozen emotion assumes a power out of proportion to its original nature. In the middle of a very harsh winter, it's wise to see to it that the water flows fairly regularly through your home plumbing system. Similarly, during the harsh seasons of grief, it is best to keep the channels open so that hurtful feelings are freely expressed. Frozen emotion, like a frozen pipe, has the potential for causing unexpected problems.

Emotions we resist can stay with us for years and years. A man I know lost his home because of a new highway construction program. The state condemned his property, and he was forced to move. Although my friend was financially compensated for his loss, he never really got over it emotionally. Instead of dealing openly with his sorrowful feelings and the bitterness he felt toward the highway department and the government officials, the man turned his anger on his wife and children. His family members couldn't understand why he was always so irritable. Work associates soon became intolerant of the man's constant cynicism and belittlement of others. He developed various aches and pains not attributable to actual physical disorder and complained to every one of his discomforts. What the man did not do was to openly grieve the loss of the home he had built with his own hands, the evergreen trees he had planted so many years before, and the many memories associated with the home that he loved.

The person who resists grieving may successfully ward off intense pain. Still, a nagging ache will likely take its place. Denied feelings of grief will be expressed in hidden ways. A low-grade depression can then endure for many years: moodiness, irritability, restlessness, nervousness, excessive use of alcohol, conflicts in relationships, physical ailments, accident proneness, reckless spending, or general dissatisfaction and disappointment with life. Grief doesn't go away just because it is ignored.

Please Don't Misunderstand

Having sat attentively through two months of one of my psychology courses, an 18-year-old student approached me in the college cafeteria. "I've been thinking about your lecture series on grief," the young man said. "And I've been working on my father."

"How do you mean?" I asked.

"Well," he replied, "you emphasized the importance of people dealing with their feelings in an open way. My father was in the war and I know he had some awful experiences. I've been working on him to get those bad memories out of his system."

Sometimes a teacher is startled to hear an unrecognizable interpretation of something that was taught in class. I was startled, all right. I was also somewhat irritated by the young man's naiveté. "Uh," I wondered aloud, "are you talking about Vietnam?"

"Yes," the young man replied. "My father was in combat. But my mother says that Dad has never been able to speak a word about it since. He gets angry whenever the subject is raised by anyone."

"Then leave your father alone," I said. I was aware that the irritation in my voice was growing. I went on talking anyway. "If your father hasn't been able to deal with whatever happened for more than 30 years, then leave him alone!"

There are many ways of surviving traumatic experiences. Some people find it essential to deny painful events. Their way of dealing with a crisis is to shut it away in a lock box. They may give unmistakable cues that they cannot directly confront a crisis. With these persons, it's important to respond to the cues, as my student should have done with his father.

Dr. Elisabeth Kübler-Ross tells a powerful story in one of her books, illustrating a situation in which denial was absolutely necessary to someone suffering from a terminal illness. A patient was receiving both radiation and chemotherapy and had read extensively about her illness. Certainly she knew that she had a serious condition, but when she asked her doctor whether it was malignant or benign, she gave the doctor no time to reply and immediately began to speak of other things. Her unspoken message was clear: "I can't handle it. I need not to know." Most medical people and family members, following such a cue from a person who is terminally ill, will allow the person to keep all denial systems intact. If the patient is obviously prepared for the truth at a later time, he or she can then be encouraged to face the crisis at hand.[2]

More commonly, it happens that a terminally ill person does indeed wish to talk honestly about his or her condition. Often family members and certain medical personnel will resist an honest sharing of the dying person's feelings of loss. They do so not to protect the dying, but to protect themselves. In any case, it is always important to take cues from the one who is grieving. What matters is whether the person *wants* to talk. What is an "appropriate death" is unique for every individual and "a single strategy, such as acceptance, is not best for every dying patient."[3]

People make use of the psychological defense mechanism of denial because it is necessary for them to do so at a certain time. We ought not to go cruelly demanding that people "get out" disturbing feelings. Rather, we should extend an invitation to talk, in an open and nonspecific way. "How are your spirits? What kind of worries do you find yourself having as you lie here in the hospital bed?" We can invite the sharing of feelings without insisting or pressuring. Saying, "I care about you" and asking a person in crisis "How are you feeling?" allows a direct reply — or a vague response.

When mourning, we respond with a deep sense of appreciation if a close friend or family member understands gentleness. We do need caring, but caring expressed without pressure. Suppose a friend of yours has the idea that you should be shedding more tears over your loss. In this event, it's a good idea to tell your friend to get off your case! If and when you are ready to cry, you will.

Many people turn to verbal expression because that's what they know best. Talking with trusted others is an effective means of releasing emotions and undergoing healing. There are, however, other ways to grieve — symbols or actions can be quite effective.

If you have a friend in a loss situation, it may be hard for you to understand that people need to work through the unsettling process of bereavement in their own ways and seasons. You may think your friend is not grieving her divorce because she has been out working in the yard every day and seems physically to be wearing herself out. How do you know that your friend isn't dealing with her feelings of anger, preoccupation with the loss, or whatever every day while she is pulling weeds and making great stacks of twigs and dry leaves in the yard?

A friend of yours may not be talking about his feelings since he lost his older brother. But have you noticed he is wearing his brother's tie clasp and is now carrying his brother's photograph? Perhaps privately, several times a day, he opens up his wallet to look at the picture. Did you know that your friend goes home at night to drill, hammer, and saw in his garage? He's building new kitchen cupboards for his dead brother's wife. He has also begun to take his brother's children to the ballpark. Your friend is indeed grieving. It would do him good to speak of his feelings of loss. But he's not going to fall over dead of a coronary for lack of talking. He is acting out his grief. You needn't be afraid to ask your friend how he is feeling or to say you're sorry for his brother's death. But don't expect him to grieve in exactly the same way that you would grieve if you lost your own brother.

Feelings, then, don't have to be expressed in a verbal and direct way. Usually grief is less prolonged when a person is able to mourn openly, through tears and an extensive spoken expression of feelings. However, what is crucial to the healing process is that some kind of catharsis takes place that enables one to reflect on the meaning of the loss and what can be learned from it.

Many women think men aren't grieving because they aren't talking. In our society, most men are still less socialized to verbal expression than are most women. Our early training being what it is, both sexes have a great deal to learn from each other about grief. Many women need to learn that there are other ways to deal with feelings than talking. Many men need to learn that verbally expressing feelings can do a lot to help a person feel better. It's important to look at the actions of someone who isn't talking before making assumptions about whether the grief process is underway.

Six days after the birth of his first child, a Down syndrome baby, an insurance salesman began to work every evening, tearing down the rickety wooden porch on the back of the couple's home. He had intended to rebuild the wooden porch anyway. Now he was tearing down the old one, piece by piece, using scarcely any tools for assistance. This young father was not resisting his grief.

Although he was able to be of emotional comfort to his wife, he was never able to put his own feelings into words. One evening after another he went out to the old porch he was rather violently disassembling. Later on he went out to the new porch he began to build. Eventually, feelings of sadness and anger were largely worked through. He began to love their baby and plan ahead for the child's special needs. His healing process was well underway.

Perhaps this couple could have become closer emotionally had the husband been able to talk about his feelings. On the other hand, perhaps he was able to share with his wife an intensified physical closeness, tenderness, and warmth. In that case, the lack of verbal communication between them didn't matter so much.

Rigorous physical activity can be a healing balm. One of the most moving stories I have ever heard was told by my friend Jane, who, like me, grew up on a farm. We often talked together about farm life and the ways people we knew there had coped with their pain. Jane related to me the story of her grandfather's death and how her father dealt with his loss. Her father, Albert, lived near his father's farm in Nebraska. A terrible fire burned the home place to the ground. It was the house where Albert was born and reared. His father burned to death inside. Jane said that everyone thought her father had "gone crazy" after the fire. Most of the other relatives were crying and talking about the tragic event. Meanwhile, Albert had borrowed a bulldozer and was bulldozing the ashes and charred remains of the house.

Rain had put the fire out the night before. Albert wasn't trying to stop the fire. He was burying the house where his father died. He worked for hours and hours, not stopping for a meal, not stopping for anything. Even when his wife begged him to come in as darkness began to fall, Albert continued to bulldoze the ground. Backward and forward. He threw the big machine into reverse and then drive. Reverse and drive. Again and again and again.

His khaki shirt was soaked with sweat. Dust found the moisture of his shirt, forming a layer of mud. Albert's face was covered with brown dust, interrupted by running lines of perspiration. His face looked like a fearsome Halloween mask.

Jane's father and grandfather were farmers. They had worked together in the fields from the time that Albert was a boy. Theirs was a nonverbal relationship, father and son. They worked together. They didn't talk about feelings.

What Albert did with his borrowed bulldozer was to grieve in the only way he knew how. Words were beyond him and so were tears. He worked the land, over and over, until the home place was completely invisible. The home and his father had been given a proper burial. The land was completely cleared and ready to be farmed. Albert would farm the land that was his father's cemetery. He could never have told you why he had to do it, why he spent the day and early night bulldozing. He himself didn't know why he did it.

Jane understood. Her father did something with his grief. Something was better than nothing. Perhaps it was the best thing he could have done.

7. THE IMPORTANCE OF SELF-CARING ACTIVITIES

To give your sheep or cow a large spacious meadow is the way to control him.

— Zen Master, Suzuki-roshi

In grief, people become oblivious to obvious things. Skills for survival and sources of comfort are overlooked. For this reason, it's important for me to stress some very basic self-care activities that can help you feel better.

Healing is a perfectly natural thing that happens in a certain atmosphere. When a person sprains an ankle playing tennis, he or she doesn't go immediately back to the tennis court, jarring the injury every day and expecting it to heal. Potentially injurious activities are avoided for a while so the natural healing process can take its course. If the weakened ankle isn't constantly forced to carry the full body's weight, the ankle will heal quite well on its own. All that is needed is a period of protection and loving care. So it is with an emotional wound.

Certain people and places are sometimes best avoided during the grieving process. A young woman painfully working through her divorce need not visit her father if he is the kind of man who will add insult to injury. "I knew that guy was a jerk all along," her father might say. "I knew 12 years ago that your marriage wouldn't work. I tried to tell your mother, but you were so bullheaded and determined to marry him anyway!"

A grieving person soon discovers that the world has an oversupply of "I told you so" people. While you are feeling emotionally bruised, avoid persons who kick you when you're down. The already blue and swollen ankle never gets well if someone stands there beating on it with a hammer.

Make up excuses. Hang up the phone. Briefly scan, then delete, or just delete the e-mail messages and notes that come from people whose words are insensitive. Tell your friend or family member that "it's just not helpful" to hear all the many ways that your suffering might supposedly have been avoided. If this doesn't work, stay away from the person as much as you can. During your time of vulnerability, it's important that you do whatever is necessary to protect yourself. You need to spend time with people who are understanding and supportive. All wounds need a nurturing atmosphere in which to heal.

The Zen saying at the beginning of this chapter implies that a sheep with all the room he needs doesn't *have* to be controlled. Provided with a rich and vast grazing land, the sheep is comfortable where he is. In the months that follow an experience of loss, human beings also need a spacious meadow with plenty of room to move about. Grieving persons who develop many resources for comfort and strength usually find that their feelings about the loss don't wander out of control.

Friends

Good friends are as basic to life and health as knowing how to cup your hands when there's nothing else to drink from. The most self-loving action any of us performs in a lifetime is learning how to develop and sustain close friendships. There are many bereavement groups you can find listed in your community newspaper or learn about from local clergy. You'll meet new friends there.

If you have several close friends, you are very fortunate. In the event that you haven't any strong friendships to rely on, you need to start now to do something about that. Reaching out to others while you are hurting is very difficult, but necessary. You can reestablish contact with old acquaintances and friends or begin to establish new friendships.

It's hard for most of us to trust others while we are feeling vulnerable. It's harder to find substitutes for the support that we need. Unless you are someone who is able to obtain great strength from nature, books, athletics, work, religion, or service to others, there just aren't many options available to you except to learn to make friends.

Some people find their closest friends among family members. With strong family ties, you may have less need for many friends outside of the family. Still, almost everyone needs additional friendships. Often when we are grief-stricken, our closest relatives have been immobilized by the same loss. Our customary resources for strength and comfort are no longer available.

If one of the partners in a love relationship becomes gravely ill, the ill partner has grief to deal with and so does the partner. A well husband may have difficulty comforting his ill wife because he is distraught and fearful of losing her. He may emotionally abandon his wife out of his anxiety over her condition. She is apt to experience his behavior as rejection and to become distraught herself. In this situation, neither partner provides the emotional support that the other needs. His grief is overwhelming. Her grief is overwhelming. In such circumstances, when love partners cannot share their separate struggles, friends outside of the family are especially important.

Many persons find it impossible to have a close friendship with someone in the family because of personality differences, strained family relations, or geographical distance. Developing bonds of trust and a feeling of closeness with non-relatives then becomes a matter of urgent necessity.

Thus, friends within the family and friends other than family are the two most essential sources of caring. If you haven't the one, you desperately need the other. Those who are willing to invest the time and undergo the struggle to have both tend to lead very satisfying lives. Suffering itself does not do us in or sabotage the will to live. Usually we sabotage ourselves by foolishly trying to live our lives in isolation. Without the comfort and love of other human beings, none of us is very strong. Aligned with others who accept us and support us, we can survive most anything.

Grieving involves searching for and pursuing those environments where healing best takes place. Achieving a sense of bonding with others requires risk-taking. Even while you are uncomfortable with sharing your pain and would prefer to remain alone, you'll need to reach out for and spend time with caring people.

In dealing with your grief, you may find that you look for comfort and friendship from one or more of the following types of people: Empathic Persons, Basic Care Providers, and Destructive People.

Empathic Persons

The Empathic Person is a good listener when you really need to talk. He or she may have different values from yours but doesn't shame you or judge you for living in your own way. This person can be fully trusted with your confidences.

A number of other traits tend to be characteristic of such a friend. The Empathic Person:

- ❖ Does not shock easily, but accepts your human feelings as human feelings.
- ❖ Is not uncomfortable with his or her own or your tears.
- ❖ Does not regularly give unwanted advice.
- ❖ Is warm and affectionate with you.
- ❖ Reminds you of your strengths when you forget that you have these strengths within yourself.
- ❖ Recognizes that you are growing.

❖ Trusts you to be able to come through your difficult time.

❖ Treats you like an adult who can make your own decisions.

❖ Acknowledges that he or she is human, too, and shares this humanness.

❖ May sometimes become impatient or angry with you, but doesn't attack your character when telling you so.

❖ Is not afraid to ask you about your loss.

❖ Respects your courage and sense of determination.

❖ Understands that grief is not a disease.

❖ Has been through troublesome times and can tell you so.

❖ May not feel comfortable with a certain feeling you are expressing, such as hate or a particular sexual yearning, but tries to understand what the feeling means to you.

❖ Tells you honestly when he or she is unable to be with you because of problems or needs of his or her own.

❖ Is faithful to commitments and promises.

Friends who are Empathic Persons can be hard to find. Many people seek the help of a psychologist, psychiatrist, clergyperson, social worker, or other counselor in order to talk with an Empathic Person. A well-trained professional is someone who listens well, with acceptance and without judgment. If more people had accepting friends capable of good listening, there would be less need for professional helpers.

You may have to look around awhile for such a friend, but you can probably discover Empathic Persons where you live and work. One thing is certain: Those who are capable of responding to your grief in an empathic way cannot be identified without risk. There is simply no other way to acquire an Empathic Person as your friend. We come close to others by risking an honest sharing of ourselves.

You may feel somewhat angry that more people haven't come to your aid. The problem may be that you haven't allowed others to become aware of your distress. Your pain cannot be understood or shared by anyone unless you allow it to be known. By gradually letting down the walls that hide your struggle, you can give selected people a chance to respond empathically to you. Try not to give up on the whole human race if the grieving feelings that you share are misunderstood by someone. You can try again until you find the friends you need.

Empathic Persons are special friends because they accept us as ourselves. They accept troublesome human feelings as a normal part of living. Usually one gets this kind of friend by being this kind of a friend.

Basic Care Providers

The Basic Care Provider worries about whether you are overworking, eating well, or taking adequate care of yourself. He or she has a gift for recognizing and responding to practical concerns that you have.

A Basic Care Provider is the kind of friend who:

- ❖ Respects your need for privacy without ignoring your need for human contact.
- ❖ Comes to your aid when practical problems arise.
- ❖ Makes you feel welcome in his or her home.
- ❖ Is thoughtful enough to include you in social activities.
- ❖ Does not encourage you in behaviors that are self-destructive.
- ❖ Volunteers to help out with tasks that are difficult for you to handle alone.
- ❖ Helps you to think things over aloud when you have a practical problem to solve.
- ❖ Expresses sensitivity to your daily needs through small acts of kindness such as looking after your car, mending your clothes, sending a gift of food, or helping out with household duties.
- ❖ Is friendly and warm toward you and treats you with respect.

❖ Anticipates days and dates that may be difficult for you and is especially thoughtful on these occasions.

❖ Treats your belongings with care.

❖ Keeps confidential whatever personal information you share.

Basic Care Providers, like Empathic Persons, create the kind of warm atmosphere in which healing occurs. While we are preoccupied with grieving, everyday problems in living can become major crises. Basic Care Providers attend to your basic needs, reducing the stress of coping with daily problems.

You may never speak directly about your loss to a Basic Care Provider. On the other hand, perhaps you will. Whatever words are said or left unsaid, it really doesn't matter. Basic Care Providers express caring for you in the practical ways that are comforting and helpful. You can receive this caring with appreciation. Such friends are made of high-quality gold.

One comes to have friends who are Basic Care Providers by getting to know the neighbors, certain relatives, the parents of your children's friends, people at work, and people whom you meet at social gatherings. By being friendly and open, initiating conversations with people, you'll come across Basic Care Providers.

Neighbors and others who are strangers can become your friends once it is clear to them that you are genuinely interested in them as persons. If you take an honest interest in the things that are important to other people, they can come to be interested in things important to you.

When people speak to you, listen to what they are telling you about values and experiences they hold dear — work, children, grandchildren, home and garden projects, pets, health concerns, travels, and perspectives on life. Some people will only talk about themselves and will never reciprocate by being attentive to your concerns. Others, if you listen well to the things they value, will be very kind to you in the ways of basic care.

Listening well means saying, "Wow, I guess that means a lot to you," and meaning it, when a neighbor tells you a touching story about her grandchild. Listening is wanting to hear. It's asking the man next door how his daughter's job search is coming along. People generally respond to those who are interested in them, and they respond with acts of kindness. Also if you are willing to become helpfully involved in others' lives in practical and thoughtful ways, you'll see plenty of caring returned to you.

Destructive People

The Destructive Person may be charming and likable. You may have shared good times and consider yourselves good friends. Yet this kind of friend somehow lacks the ability to support and to care. He or she may be jealous and resentful of you, or may be too focused on himself or herself to sense your needs.

The Destructive Person may harm you and complicate your mourning in a wide variety of ways. He or she:

* Tells others things you intended to have kept in confidence.
* Fails to repay money borrowed from you or to return your belongings.
* Responds to you in ways that are poorly timed or somehow unsettling.
* Tells you stories of tragedies and catastrophe when you are feeling vulnerable.
* Makes light of things sacred or meaningful to you.
* Continually questions you and your decisions.
* Makes apparent to you his or her disapproval of other people's behavior, which resembles yours.
* Speaks repeatedly of subjects that are painful to you.

❖ Continues behaviors that you've made clear directly harm and upset you.

❖ Fails to follow through on promises.

❖ Habitually uses alcohol to excess or abuses other drugs and encourages you to do the same.

❖ Labels your feelings or behavior as "silly," "sick," "weird," "crazy," "hysterical," "abnormal," "childish," "stupid," "lazy," "selfish," or "feeling sorry for yourself."

No one is helped by having a primary relationship with a Destructive Person. Especially if the "friend" is more consistently destructive than caring and helpful, you need to ask yourself why you are continuing the relationship. It is a self-destructive act on your part to place yourself repeatedly in settings that are alien to healing. You may think that you must tolerate the punishments of a Destructive Person because no one else would care for you. Perhaps it will help you to remember that Destructive Persons can only intensify your hurt and prolong your grief.

There are many good people in the world, people who can become available to you. Many Empathic Persons and Basic Care Providers are awaiting discovery. Go find them.

Sometimes your friends will need you to set aside your mourning in order to be available for helping them. Most good friendships and love relationships are like this. People take turns.

One of the things to watch out for in choosing friends is that you don't overlook some of the finest people around. A person who seems a most unlikely candidate for friendship may become your closest friend. A potential friend may be someone very different from you in religious and social background, interests, personality, and educational level. There are 20-year-olds with the sensitivity of an experienced 40-year-old. Some 80-year-olds are more flexible, open-minded, and understanding than any young person you will meet. Good friends are to be found in all kinds of places and in all age groups. If you've discovered this fact already, you're either really lucky or really smart.

In the first year after the loss of my husband through divorce, I shared many weekends with friends. Although I felt like staying home and withdrawing inwardly, I made myself visit friends in towns and cities both distant and near. Once there, I was always glad.

Bill served me from an endless supply of compassion. Peg and I took long walks together; she praised my homemade bread. Catherine and my adoptive grandmother, Miss Amy, shared stories of their lives in India as we picnicked in the backyard. With Steven and Naomi, I enjoyed the special holidays. With Marian and Blake, I shared many tears and lots of card games. With Eleanor and Frank, there were Sunday dinners and times of sharing. With Al, Cherry, Judy, and also Dorris, good talks.

During the good and bad times in my life, I've looked to exercise as a source of strength. With Beverly and her twin brothers, with Bob and Gretchen, or with my local women's league, I've played tennis. With Norma and Jack or Romaine, I've played golf. With Marian, Janyne, Linda and Burt, Jan, Kim, and others, there were and still are long walks and talks. Without close friends, a period of professional counseling, lots of exercise, and meaningful work to do, I can't imagine how I could have gotten through mourning the loss by suicide of two people I loved. Sometimes I talked about my feelings of loss with my friends, but mostly I turned to them as people who would love and accept me. I was not constantly catered to or treated like a wounded bird. When sleep wouldn't come, there were snacks to eat and newspapers to read. I could talk with my friends when I most needed to talk. In my situation, it also was necessary to be a useful family member, not always preoccupied with my grief. People took an interest in my work and ongoing life. These good people virtually saved my life.

Friends help to remind us not to discount the realm of the ordinary in our sorrow. Everyday activities shared with others provide strength.

Companionship is healing. There is solace in athletic activities, card playing, concerts, movies, a college course, a good book, meals and drinks shared, and interesting conversation. Activity itself can be a healer.

There are many bereavement groups you can find listed in your community newspaper or learn about from local clergy. You'll meet new friends there. It is important to remember, however, that we all have different personalities and coping styles. Some people are more private, tend to withdraw inward during bad times, and are content with being alone in good times. What matters is the degree to which one feels engaged in a healing process. If you feel stuck in depression or other troublesome feelings, you need to get out of the house and among caring people.

Sexual Needs

While grieving, many of us find it necessary to meet our emotional needs in ways that those close to us and even we ourselves may not understand.

Robin, a recently divorced woman, had a sexual encounter with a man who was an acquaintance. It was a first date, spur-of-the-moment decision about which Robin felt very guilty afterwards. I was a chaplain at the time at the university where Robin was a student, and it was obvious why she presented herself to me. Robin's entire manner reflected embarrassment and announced her yearning for acceptance and understanding as a needful human being. Robin said that she had never before slept with a man other than her husband. For several months she had felt profoundly depressed, she recalled, and was preoccupied with the fear that no man would ever find her lovable or attractive. An unhappy marriage and destructive divorce had left her desperate for caring.

Looking glum and ashamed to be telling me about her affair, Robin sat in my office awaiting a response from me. She said they had gone to a motel and that she had felt cheap "signing in with him there, as if we were a couple of sneaky teenagers." Watching Robin's face and listening to her words, I was thinking that one doesn't rebuild a life that has been broken down without receiving from others some form of tenderness. I asked Robin if she had been tender with the man and if he had been tender with her. She nodded her head affirmatively. I then asked, "What is so cheap about a man and a woman bringing comfort to each other in this way?" She had no reply.

"You can punish yourself for your humanness," I said, "by deciding that tenderness is a prostitution if it takes place in a motel. The other alternative is to accept yourself as having met your needs in the best way you could at the time."

Many grieving people feel guilty about their sexual behavior, particularly behavior that is a departure from the person's previous way of life. A bereaved man or woman, for example, may begin regularly to masturbate for the first time or may masturbate much more frequently than usual. Many fear that this behavior represents personal inadequacy, moral wrongdoing, or a failure to cope with the loss in a healthy way. Never are any of these unfortunate interpretations of masturbatory activity appropriate to the situation of the bereaved person.

People who are grieving are people who are hurting. As is true of a host of other coping behaviors in a time of crisis, masturbation is seldom harmful and often brings comfort and a release from tension. Years ago as a doctoral student, I remember seeing a study indicating that "25 percent of 70-year-old women still masturbate" and that both men and women, including elderly persons, tend to remain sexually responsive as a result of continued sexual activity.[1] This means that partners separated by circumstances, divorced persons, and widowed people who masturbate when without a partner are more likely to retain sexual responsiveness when reunited than are persons who were sexually inactive for long periods of time. Kinsey found that girls and young women who had engaged in masturbatory activity prior to marriage were more sexually responsive and sexually satisfied in marriage than girls and young women who had not masturbated.[2] Masturbation is simply not the so-called "indication of maladjustment" that people unfamiliar with research findings on the subject commonly believe it to be. Furthermore, for many hurting persons, sexual release through masturbation is a profound comfort, which often benefits the healing process.

While neither masturbation nor an affair offers the ultimate solution for a person who is suffering inner pain, sexual activity helps many people through the pilgrimage. In my opinion, it's unkind and cruel to condemn a behavior that may simply represent part of one's effort to survive unless the behavior harms or threatens someone. Across the lifespan, sexuality is simply part of our humanity. Writes Dr. Herbert Gingold in *The National Psychologist*, people of all ages (including seniors) can "benefit from knowing that flirtation, masturbation, sexual activity and sexual fantasy are all normal experiences."[3]

Avoiding Major Decisions

When one is facing a significant loss, generally the first year of bereavement is not the time for significant decisions. Unless unusual circumstances require doing so, this is not the time to move to a strange city, change jobs, remarry, have elective surgery, buy a new home, or make any other major decisions. Ordinarily, it is also not the time for deciding to have a child or deciding to bring someone else into your family.

A grieving person is one whose judgment is clouded. Depending on the nature and severity of your loss, impairment in judgment can be expected for at least a few months and usually longer.

Lynn Caine, the author of the book *Widow*, describes what she terms her "crazy period" in the first year of bereavement:

> Within three months after Martin died, I had given up our comfortable apartment in Manhattan, bought a house I hated across the river in Hackensack, New Jersey, pulled the children out of their New York schools and enrolled them in new suburban schools, embraced a way of life that did not appeal to me, that I was not suited for, could not afford and could not cope with. I was absolutely irresponsible and crazy. And even today I can't explain exactly what was going through my head.
>
> ...My frenzy of activity, my moving, my refusal to listen to the friends who said "Take it easy" — all of this, I am convinced, was a frantic postponement of the moment I would have to face widowhood. Perhaps if I had understood the forces at work, I could have accepted that wise advice everyone gave me: "Don't make a move." But how is a widow to know that she is not in control? The answer, I have learned, is that you don't have to know. Just take it on faith. You are *not* in control. No matter what you think.
>
> And so I moved. Into a pretty little suburban box with green in front and a stone wall in the back. It had a picture window, the bus stop was around the corner and there was a basement where the children could play on rainy days. I hated it. As soon as the moving van left, I knew I had made a terrible mistake.[4]

Regret is a very difficult emotion with which to live. In grief, it's almost always best to choose a conservative course, to move slowly and carefully. Some choices are irrevocable.

Alvin Toffler, in his classic book *Future Shock*, described the human animal as highly adaptable to change but not infinitely adaptable. In the transitional periods of our lives marked by sudden and dramatic change, we greatly need what Toffler terms "stability zones."[5] It's essential to our mental stability to maintain routines, to fly the machine in a holding pattern as much as possible.

For more than four decades two researchers, Thomas Holmes and Richard Rahe, along with their associates, have studied change and its effect on people's psychological and physical health. What they have confirmed is that too much change within a two-year period literally makes people sick. Life stress can lead to health problems, whether the change is positive (marriage, a promotion, moving to a new home), or negative (the loss of a loved one, being fired from a job, foreclosure on a mortgage, a significant decrease in income), or something in between (a son or daughter going off to college, gaining a new family member). When too much change takes place in too short a time, our chances of becoming ill increase significantly.[6]

For college students, trouble with a roommate, failing a course, or applying to graduate school are stressful events often linked to illness.[7] For African-American students there is greater stress than for white Americans from such events as major changes in work responsibilities or living conditions or a major personal injury.[8]

Areas of your life that you can stabilize are best held as "safety zones" now. You may already be suffering from a change in your sleeping and eating habits, recreational and social activities, and living conditions. In general, major decisions that would produce still more change should be delayed.

Anticipating Difficult Days and Dates

It can be helpful to know in advance that you will feel more unhappy and lonely on certain days and dates than at other times. Planning ahead for these occasions is very important. It's one of the ways that you can take care of yourself.

Depending on your own situation, some days will be especially difficult: your birthday, the birthday of your lost loved one, your wedding or anniversary, the anniversary of the death date or other loss, graduations, Mother's Day, Father's Day, Thanksgiving, Christmas, Easter, Hanukkah, Passover, Eid al-Fitr, Eid al-Adha, or other holidays on which there are traditional meals and families are together. You may find that you dread the day or date, even dread the entire month in which a particular date is on the calendar.

Try to remember well ahead of time the days that will be charged with intense emotion. On these days, you can plan to be with close friends or with family members who are kind and understanding. You are likely to feel tearful or depressed on these occasions more than at any other time. You will need to be in the company of others, preferably people who care about you.

Holidays, special days, and weekends are the worst times to be alone. Some people find that it helps them more to go to work than to be with family and friends. Others schedule themselves for useful volunteer activities, such as "Meals on Wheels" or serving at a soup kitchen for homeless people. The most important thing is to be certain not to get caught without having made specific plans.

If you are the friend of someone who has suffered a loss, remember the special dates that will be difficult for your friend. These are ideal occasions for acts of kindness — a phone call, a card or letter, a gift of flowers or food dropped by the house, a personal visit, or an invitation to your house. Don't be afraid to talk honestly to your grieving friend: "I wanted to write this note because I know that on Sunday it will be a year since John died. Probably the day will be very painful for you. I just want you to know that I'm thinking of you and that I love you."

People are afraid to speak candidly with grieving persons for fear that the bereaved one will be upset by direct comments. It's the idea that if we don't remind our friend of her loss a year ago, she won't be thinking of it. This notion is unrealistic to the point of being ridiculous. Of course she knows what day it is. Wouldn't you, if a loved one of yours had died a year ago today?

Amy was a young artist who lived next door to me in East Lansing, Michigan. After her mother died in November, she lived alone with her father. On Mother's Day, six months after her mother's death, I saw Amy out in the yard cutting flowers. I walked over and said, "Hi, I just thought I'd come over and talk for a while. I know that it's your first Mother's Day without your mother, and it's probably a tough day."

Tears came into Amy's eyes as she blurted out an immediate response to my words. "You're the first person all day who has even mentioned Mother's Day," she exclaimed. "Doesn't anyone know that I know it's Mother's Day and that I miss her?"

Amy was comfortable with my having acknowledged her feelings. I did not make her cry or upset her. Her tears were appreciative tears. Someone was finally paying attention to the sad feelings and memories already stirring inside. Amy had long dreaded the arrival of Mother's Day. From the time that Mother's Day gift displays began appearing everywhere in store windows, she had had an uneasy feeling. My words were a kind acknowledgment, not a cruel reminder.

When a friend is grieving, try not to ignore the obvious. Straight talk is a much more appreciated and sensitive response than avoidance.

When you are the one who is grieving and your well-meaning friends avoid mentioning the loss, remind them what day it is. Ask for help in a direct way: "I really need to talk about what I'm feeling today." Or, if you don't feel like talking, explain why and ask for their understanding.

The first year is the hardest. Every special calendar date comes up for the first time since the loss. In subsequent years, you will still need to take care of yourself by planning activities well ahead for special dates, holidays, and weekends. Usually the need for planned activity is not as pronounced as time goes on, but it's still important. The sting may linger for several years.

Expecting Unexpected Trouble

Perhaps six months, a year and a half, or three years have gone by since your loss. Already you have passed through many of the phases of grief. You are feeling much better and your ability to concentrate is intact. You are able to work and play and once again enjoy living. You continue to think of your loss on occasion, but it has been quite a while since you've felt deeply troubled over it.

Now that you think you are home free, that the worst of the pain is over, you may find yourself getting sad or tearful unexpectedly. A movie may send you into a depressed mood. An argument may erupt with someone at work or home. Perhaps a conflict in a new love relationship or friendship will provoke a replay of old, intense wounded feelings.

Dr. Carr, who was angry at becoming pregnant while she was faithfully using birth control (see Chapter 5), had her abortion and sought professional counseling to deal with her mixed feelings. She mourned the necessity of the abortion, as she saw it, as a choice between her medical career and a family. She struggled with guilt, anger, and sadness. For several months she talked with her therapist about the man by whom she had become pregnant and her sorrow that their relationship had ended without his being able to share her troublesome feelings about the abortion. She seemed to make peace with her circumstances, felt that her work as a medical resident was again up to par, and terminated her psychotherapy sessions. Things went along fine until Dr. Carr completed her residency, set up her own medical practice, and fell in love again. Finding herself in a new relationship with a man quite different from the man she had loved before, Dr. Carr still found the two men alike in her own mind. The abortion issue came up again as she found herself mistrusting her new lover and men in general on the basis of the previous hurtful experience. Uneasy feelings also came up again whenever the public debate over abortion was aired on television or in the newspapers. Finally, as she reached a comfortable level of financial security following several years of private practice, Dr. Carr began to mourn her childless state and began to experience a renewed sadness over having had to give up her pregnancy. She wondered what it would be like now to have a five-year-old child, and she returned for a time to her previous therapist to talk about these feelings.

Recovery from loss is like having to get off the main highway every so many miles because the direct route is under reconstruction. The road signs reroute you through little towns you hadn't expected to visit and over bumpy roads you hadn't wanted to bounce around on. You are basically traveling in the appropriate direction. On the map, however, the course you are following has the look of shark's teeth instead of a straight line. Although you are gradually getting there, you are sometimes in doubt that you will ever again get back to the finished highway.

8. A Slow Readjustment Back to Life and Work

Work is the closest thing to sanity.

— Sigmund Freud

It doesn't make any sense. You bury your father on one day and your employer expects you back at work on the next day. If you're a student, you're due back at school. As a homemaker, you're supposed to continue your responsibilities at home.

A family member is suffering from a terminal illness and your work is supposed to continue as usual. You have sick leave days, but you're not sick; someone else is. So you continue to work. Or your marriage has ended and you feel devastated about it. Others expect you to fulfill your normal work responsibilities, day after day. You go right on doing the laundry, spending time with the children, preparing meals, making a living, and paying the bills.

After a major emotional loss of almost any kind, people expect us to continue the activities of life and work. It doesn't make any personal emotional sense, but it makes some practical sense. There are benefits to living in a world where people expect certain things of us. Activity is a crucial ingredient of the healing process. The whole idea of "keeping busy" is both absolutely crazy and absolutely necessary.

Because mourning is characterized by a long period of depression, mobilizing yourself for activity will probably be very difficult. Work and other activities you once pursued with interest may now be drudgery.

87

Especially in the early months, just getting up in the morning and sending yourself off to the job may seem to require all the strength that you have. Just to prepare a meal or complete some small daily task can represent a major accomplishment. By definition, depression is a sad mood accompanied by a lowering of vitality, a reduction in the amount and quality of activity, and the tendency to fatigue easily. For most people, depression is the main feature of grieving and it requires the longest struggle. Although the intensity and constancy of your depression should diminish as time goes on, you are apt to have some difficult bouts of depression for at least a year. Depressed periods less severe may continue for a longer time.

Time Away from Work

No employer expects an employee to resume a full workload immediately after major surgery. It is commonly expected, however, that an employee will function as usual when he or she has suffered a major loss. This distinction that is made by our cultural institutions regarding physical and emotional suffering is both distressing and interesting.

The American culture is a society of "doers and achievers." We are a production-oriented culture. Today, whether family leave time is mandated by law or allowed by some employers, society still values a man on the job, for example, more than leave time for a father with a sick child. Frequently, women are disparagingly described as "unstable" workers for being more prone than men to stay home with an ill family member.

Employers usually have firm guidelines as to what are the acceptable and unacceptable causes of an absence from work. Physical illnesses are regarded as legitimate reasons for not "doing and achieving," but the emotional needs of ourselves and our loved ones often are not similarly regarded as legitimate.

We pay a price for this production-oriented value system. The quality of our life together as a human community is impaired. By providing workers with so little time away from work to attend to emotional and family needs, we undermine family and friendship bonds and undermine our own psychological health as well.

Occasions will arise which call for your being absent from work not because you are physically ill, but because your spirit is in need of time to repair itself. It is important for you to recognize these occasions when a day or a few days off are needed. Especially in the first three to six months of bereavement, you are likely to need a day of freedom from work now and then. Perhaps your boss is one who will understand this necessity for periodic "mental health day" absences during your grieving period. If not, you may need to take sick leave. Working is one of the most effective ways to maintain mental stability in a time of stress, yet it is equally important not to overwork and occasionally to have time away from work.

In our culture grieving people who are "taking it well" are admired and rewarded with social praise. This attitude is unfortunate, since many who supposedly are doing so well really aren't. Rarely is behaving as if no loss has occurred the good sign it is often believed to be. Most people only gradually regain an ability to pursue a normal level of activities. It's not an indication of character weakness to take several days off when a major loss first occurs and then to take an occasional respite when one is needed.

Daily Routines

Prolonged inactivity leads people to repeat the depressive stages of grief over and over again, to no benefit. Resuming a normal schedule of work activities as soon as possible is the best thing that you can do. However, if you expect yourself to work with your normal energy level and ability to concentrate, you are placing an inhuman demand on yourself. In the first six to twelve months, your mental and physical competencies will simply not be up to par. Depending on the nature of your loss, you may not resume your full powers of functioning for as long as two or three years.

Daily routines bring stability during the transition periods of our lives. Lynn Caine, in her book *Widow*, offers good advice: "Keep your job if you have one, and find one if you don't. Even if you have children that need you, get a job. A part-time job, a volunteer job, anything that will provide you with a routine and stability."[1]

Survivors of 9/11 who lost their jobs in the terrorist attack on the World Trade Center in 2001 suffered higher rates of depression for the very reason that going on with our work is how most of us keep our lives structured enough to cope with trauma. Those with a low level of social support or who lost a friend or relative during the events also had a higher likelihood of depression. Probably because of a lingering cultural reluctance to seek help, Hispanic males who lived near the towers had higher rates of post-traumatic stress (PTSD) and depression than other ethnic groups. Having two or more prior stressors or having a panic attack during or shortly after the traumatic events similarly increased vulnerability to PTSD and severe depression.[2]

Almost regardless of your circumstance of loss, work has an extremely therapeutic value. Having to be responsible to other people will help you to mobilize your inner strength. Just remember to have the compassion toward yourself to know and accept your human limits. Your work performance will only gradually return to a normal level.

Praising yourself for what you are able to do is a much kinder way to go about the recovery process than is self-belittlement. Try not to become impatient over your impaired functioning and the fact that often you don't feel like working. Many days you'll be going to work despite not feeling up to it, simply because you know it's a help to your own healing process.

You probably wouldn't yell at a little child who is cranky because he or she has had a high fever for a week and is weary from it. A wise parent would say to the child, "You're just not feeling your regular self. What activities can we think of that would help you to feel better?" Children in distress aren't the only people who need to be addressed with kind words. Grownups can profit from learning to talk with themselves in a loving way. When we are hurting, each of us has a little girl or little boy inside of us, a fragile part of ourselves that needs understanding. Practical remedies of some kind are needed for comfort.

If you absolutely must remain at home most of the time, a schedule of daily and weekly activities is especially important. Try to follow a schedule as much as you can, even if at first you can only bring yourself to complete one planned activity per day: doing the laundry, shopping for groceries, spending an hour straightening the house, taking a long walk. Every week, preferably on the same day or days of the week, plan to get out of the house one way or another. You can arrange a regular child-watching exchange with a friend or family member if that is needed. At least for a few hours on a regular weekly basis you need time away from home with other adults.

The value of physical activity cannot be overemphasized, particularly activity that helps you to organize and order your life. Under stress, many people have an intensified need for organization and structured time. It will comfort you to structure more orderliness, cleanliness, and attractiveness into your physical surroundings — especially if you do the work yourself. Physical activity is the most difficult type of activity to undertake while you are feeling depressed and are lacking in energy, but it is also probably the most therapeutic.

Try to do something for someone else, something that helps you to feel useful. Take care that you don't overextend yourself. At the same time, commit yourself to something and stick to it. Regularly pursuing an activity of benefit to another person, even while you're hurting, will help you to respect yourself.

Small acts of self-caring have always been extremely helpful to me in times of duress. Taking a warm bath at bedtime, changing from bed clothes into regular clothes first thing in the morning, having a dog to care for and take for walks, working out at the gym or getting a manicure, setting the table attractively even when eating alone, sitting outside for a while when the weather is nice, regularly buying a small bouquet of cut flowers — even such small things can help you to feel better.

After the earlier period of grief has passed, finding a group to join that fits your particular age, sex, life situation, and interests can also be helpful. A community center, athletic club, local college, or your church or synagogue may offer a group activity that you would enjoy. There are many groups based on hobbies or special interests. A friend of mine volunteers for the Service Corps of Retired Executives (SCORE). Another friend belongs to the National Puzzlers League and another is active in a beading society where creative people share, learn, and make lovely jewelry. Depressed people don't feel like pursuing self-caring activities. You'll have to prod yourself into it until regular routines are established.

The Awful Kindnesses of Others

As no doubt you have already discovered, many people haven't any idea how to respond helpfully to your situation of loss. Your slow readjustment back to life and work has probably been made *slower* by the awful kindnesses of certain friends, family members, and work associates.

My friend Jane separated from her husband a year ago. Extremely unhappy in her marriage, Jane had been writing her escape plan for several years. She would finish her education, have a way to support herself, and then leave her husband. He was unaware that she was planning to leave.

By the time Jane followed through with her decision, she could no longer tolerate her husband's verbal abuse and his open affairs with other women. She had considered leaving him for so long and so carefully that her action gave her a sense of self-respect and well-being.

Two months after she filed for divorce, Jane ran into an old friend whom she hadn't seen in quite some time. "I understand that you've left your husband," her friend Carlton said. "How are you?"

"Well," Jane replied. "I'm doing okay. Some days are rough; but I made a decision that for me was the best."

"You are denying what you feel!" Carlton exclaimed. "You must be feeling miserable, so miserable that you're just not facing it."

Jane was astonished. She had expected her old friend to be more sympathetic. "Carlton," she said, "that's *not* how I'm feeling!"

"Oh yes it is, Jane," Carlton replied, raising his voice. "Divorced women don't know what their feelings are. They often think they're happy and really they're not."

"Look, Carlton," she said, trying again. "I'm really feeling pretty good about it. The last four years of my marriage were very unhappy. I'm glad it's over."

"Sheer denial," Carlton retorted, repeating himself. Apparently, he was the kind of fellow who had to have the last word. Jane was seeing a side of him that she had never seen before. It was a curious interchange. Jane walked away from Carlton feeling angry but also confused. "This guy offers an absolute refusal to listen to me," she thought to herself. "He asked me how I was. Then he tried to tell me how I was and acted as if I should be grateful for it!"

For quite a number of days, Jane found herself swimming in a mood of restlessness and confusion. "My gosh," she wondered, "maybe he's right. Am I only fooling myself? Do I think I'm happy but actually I'm feeling miserable?" Carlton's words provoked a setback in the progress Jane was making in her grief process. She had already been through the "feeling miserable" stage. Those unhappy feelings consumed her years before when she first began planning her divorce. Now she was past that. "Carlton doesn't know what the hell he's talking about," Jane finally decided. Still, several weeks went by before she regained a sense of confidence about her decision.

David, a man who lost his father and his best friend in the same year, put into words the sentiment that Jane and many other persons have expressed. "While I grieved, every damn body became an expert on grief and what I felt. Everybody had the answer. Those who knew the least became the experts."

Not everyone misunderstands our grief, of course. Some of our loved ones manage to find just the right words of comfort. I remember my sister's phone call from Texas just after the end of my marriage. "I guess you feel like you're a hundred years old," she said. Her words touched me deeply. What she said was exactly how I felt. I was 28, feeling very tired and old. My sister expressed her empathy toward me by finding tender words.

Inevitably, some family members and friends, like Carlton, will impose their own values and interpretations on your unique situation. When you need not to cry, some friends will say, "Why aren't you crying? You should cry!" At other times, while the tears flow, friends will say, "You've got to quit this crying; you're going to have a nervous breakdown if you keep it up!"

By the way, people don't have "nervous breakdowns" from crying. As a matter of fact, there is no such thing in psychology and psychiatry textbooks as a "nervous breakdown." The expression is popular among laypersons. In most people's minds, the term means "going crazy." This notion couldn't be farther from the truth. People seldom become mentally ill simply because they are under stress. Other factors usually come into play such as a family history of mental illness, a disease process of some kind, or a toxic reaction to alcohol or other drugs. When a little child is hurt and cries and cries, it never occurs to the child to think, "Oh gosh, I'm having a nervous breakdown!" Such a concept is an adult construct and a completely false one. Crying usually helps people to feel better. What crying *doesn't* mean is that the weeping person is "falling apart." Whether you feel comfortable or uncomfortable with tears, you should follow what feels helpful to you. Don't allow a long grieving process to become longer still by listening to the well-meant but unhelpful advice of others.

When my mother was in the last few days of her life, one of the hospice nurses interpreted my mother's agitation and confusion as a "battle with the Devil." Having taught many wonderful medical people who would never presume to say such a thing and loving my mother so much, I was furious! Our mother was the closest person my sister, brother, and I have ever known to having the heart of a saint. Waging a battle with evil was not what she would be needing to do on her way out of this life! I insisted that the nurse get my mother's physician on the phone right then. Thankfully, he prescribed the medicine needed to treat the psychosis that sometimes accompanies the dying process, and my mother was able to rest.

Well-intentioned friends and family members frequently are known to say offensive things that have to do with religion. Nothing is more abrasive in a time of sorrow than having someone impose on us his or her religious interpretations. If you happen to believe that your loved one's death, your divorce, your illness, or the birth of your handicapped child was God's will, that is one thing. If you don't believe that God works in this way, it will infuriate you to hear such an interpretation of your loss. In the latter case, you may have to tell your friend, "Look, that's not how I see it. Don't tell me that my loss happened because it was in God's plan!"

Similarly, a friend may say about your loss that "it's for the best." That's all right if it happens to represent your own feeling. It's an unhelpful comment in other circumstances. "I feel so sorry for you" is probably the worst thing that can be said. Clearly this friend or family member is scrambling for words. No grieving person wants pity. That's why we say we are "paying our respects" by going to the funeral home or making a condolence call. Respect, compassion, and empathy, not pity, are what we need.

Another unhelpful remark is the expression, "You just have to keep going." A newly divorced or widowed person left with children to raise doesn't need to hear this comment. She or he knows better than anyone else the challenges that lie ahead. A friend who has the insensitivity to say what this grieving parent already painfully realizes may provoke considerable anger. A more helpful response would be, "I guess you feel like you are having to find strengths within yourself you didn't know you had."

When parents mourn a miscarriage or stillbirth, it is not uncommon for certain medical people or family members to say, "You can be thankful that you have other children," or "You can get pregnant again." As one group studying the parents of stillborns has written, "These parents do not want 'other' children — they grieve for the loss of a particular child.[3]

Popular, too, is the comment made to teenagers and younger adults who have lost a love: "You're young. You'll fall in love again." That's like telling someone immediately after losing their beloved 12-year-old dog to just go get another one. Maybe it does help to get another dog to love before you feel completely ready. Commonly, however, when a human love is lost through death or the breakup of a relationship, one wonders whether he or she will ever love again. Feelings of loss last for quite some time. Rosy prophecies of the future won't help. When we are hurting, we want others to take our present grief seriously.

Some people will tell us that a lot of people have the type of problem we have or that many have worse problems. What they are doing is minimizing our experience, often engendering our resentment in the process. It is true that what is called "downward comparison" (knowing others whose sorrows are greater) can lift us out of our less severe feelings of depression. But usually we feel better when we look around at others' suffering and think such thoughts on our own, not when someone seems to be judging us.

Awful kindnesses retard the grieving process more than move it along. Sometimes we need to tell our friend or family member what is helpful to us and what is not: "I just can't handle it when you say [this or that]." or "It would be more helpful for you to respond to me [in this way]."

Only within the last few decades in the United States have there been significant efforts to provide grief education to laypersons and helping professionals. Death and bereavement courses have been initiated all over the country in hospitals, colleges, high schools, community organizations, and religious institutions. Finally, the grieving process is being widely discussed. There is now more openness toward the subjects of death and grief.

Still, however, many Americans don't understand the healing process and have difficulty responding helpfully to one who is grieving. Strong family, friendship, and community ties are needed to provide the comfort that bereaved people require.

9. Unusually Prolonged Grief

There is no grief which time does not lessen and soften.

— Cicero

In the early aftermath of a significant loss, one commonly feels that he or she can never again be satisfied with life. Normally, this is a feeling that diminishes with the passage of time.

Many mourners suffer from episodes of depression, despair, and regressive setbacks for well over two years, and later they make exceptionally good adaptations to a new life.[1] On the one hand, episodes of depression and periodic setbacks are to be expected. On the other hand, a long-standing inability to cope with the loss signals trouble.

Mr. Morinski, the uncle of one of my students, was never the same after his wife died. After nine years had passed, his dead wife's clothes still hung in the closets. Not a piece of furniture was moved. Everything in the home remained as it had been when his wife was alive. A retired plumber, Mr. Morinski became something of a recluse once he was living alone. He rarely visited friends, never took a vacation, and seldom left his home except to shop for basic necessities. Although he was in good physical health, Mr. Morinski's yard work and occasional visits with his niece were the only activities in which he maintained interest.

Generally speaking, when the mourning process consumes a person in this way for longer than two years, the primary problem is not the loss event itself, but something else. As the years went by, Mr. Morinski's problem was not the fact that his wife had died. His main difficulty concerned the extent of his dependency on his wife while she was alive and his inability gradually to develop a life of his own after her death.

Cherishing a lost loved one's belongings and permanently holding on to some of them as precious reminders is normal behavior. Regarding *every* belonging, piece of clothing, or furniture arrangement as sacred for more than a year or so is not a typical grief reaction. In the latter instance, grief has become something other than grief.

A friend of mine moved into a new home with her husband-to-be. She found that the draperies he was hanging in their bedroom were from the bedroom of his first marriage. Sarah came to me because she was troubled with the idea that the man she was planning to marry was "still living in the past." I asked Sarah what else Marvin had brought with him from his first marriage. She replied that he had brought the cat and just a few other things. "Are the drapes pretty?" I asked. "Yes," she said, "they're very nice and colorful." I told Sarah that it seemed to me that Marvin simply liked the draperies. I also said that it was probably a very good thing that he was emotionally able to take along with him into their relationship some nice material things from his first marriage. "It's good," I said, "that he doesn't feel a need to throw away everything that represents the past." However, if Marvin was still wearing the silk pajamas his ex-wife had given him, that would be another matter!

Healthy grieving does not involve a denial of the past any more than it involves a refusal to embrace the future. It is important that we take along with us what was good about the past, as a new future slowly is created. Taking the good along with us is not the same thing as never leaving behind what has been lost.

Sarah's husband-to-be had successfully completed an emotional separation from his first wife. On the day that Sarah became upset as Marvin hung the draperies, he had tried to explain to her that his commitment was now with the new relationship. It wasn't necessary, he told her, to cast aside the past entirely in order to live in the present. Mr.

Morinski, on the other hand, was never able to face the full reality of his wife's death. He continued to live with all of her belongings around him as if any day she might return.

Severe forms of grieving occur when the mourner was excessively dependent on the one who died,[2] when guilt is a strong component of the grieving person's loss or basic characterological makeup, and for a variety of other reasons. For some people, grief and suffering have become a way of life as opposed to being a process that is necessary but temporary.

Atonement Themes

Atonement is the attempt to make up for something we think we've done wrong. A little child who feels remorse for a real or perceived wrong that has gone unnoticed may begin to get into trouble as a way of obtaining punishment and "atoning" for the wrong. Adults in distress, when it comes to matters of guilt and atonement, aren't so different from children in this way. Unresolved guilt is an emotion powerful enough to cause us to bring suffering upon ourselves.

Guilt can render us more vulnerable to psychological disturbances or can lead to an impairment in our physical health. Some people cease caring for themselves adequately and fall ill when struggling with feelings of guilt. Unresolved guilt can also cause us to sabotage our own best interests by unduly prolonging the grieving process. In other words, sometimes grief is prolonged because the mourner feels it ought to be.

Lily Pincus, in her book *Death and the Family*, tells the story of the hard-working wife who dutifully manages the daily life of her home and family, "who keeps herself, her home and her children, meticulously clean and runs from one authority to another to complain of her dirty, drunken husband." On the one hand, says social worker Pincus, this frantic woman was seeking reassurance from doctors, social workers, clergy, and the like that she was good and her husband was bad. On the other hand, she unknowingly yearned to have her own "bad and dirty side" accepted by someone she respected. Had the alcoholic husband died, the woman's grief might have been characterized by intense guilt because she could never take back all the times she announced to her children and others that her husband was a "swine of a father, lying drunk in the gutter."

The main character in this case history was not the perfect person she professed herself to be; and her husband was not the horrible beast she presented him as. Yet she attributed to him all of his weaknesses and all of her own as well. When eventually she grieves her husband's death, the great guilt that is present in her unconscious mind may lead to long and excessive mourning.[3]

Psychologically, this story is a complicated account that presents the concept of *negative projection*. Negative projection means that we attribute to others those traits in ourselves that are unacceptable or repugnant to us. If we accomplish an "overkill" in our negative projections so that another person's reputation in the community is harmed by our public words or actions, we may feel guilty when death or tragedy befalls the person. Unduly extended bereavement becomes a way of inflicting self-punishment for this situation.

Another prime example of how guilt can lead to excessive mourning is a situation involving life insurance money. Natalie's husband was a popular principal of a junior high school. After he died in an airplane crash on school business, his wife and infant son were left with a huge life insurance policy to protect them. Two years had passed since her young husband died when Natalie came for counseling. Looking older than her 25 years, she complained of depression and intense feelings of guilt. She had "never had life so easy" financially, she said, and she felt that it was all "death money."

Worried that her son would grow up without a father, Natalie had found a man to date who was extremely loving toward the baby and toward her. But she felt guilty. "The insurance money is enough for the baby and me to live on for the rest of our lives," she explained. "So it's wrong of me ever to fall in love with another man."

Natalie felt that she would never be able to take off her wedding ring. "I can't be left with all this money and live as if I'm not still married to him," she said. If she ever did remarry, Natalie told me, her new husband would have to understand that she would wear two wedding bands and "always be married to two men."

When feelings of guilt remain unresolved, grieving people commonly make an unconscious effort to atone for their real or imagined wrongs. Atonement can take the form of self-sacrifice, self-denial, or self-imposed suffering. In Natalie's case, she was atoning chiefly by pursuing career goals in a self-destructive, self-sabotaging pattern of behavior. Eighteen months after her husband's death, she enrolled in nursing school and began to sabotage her every effort to succeed. She provoked arguments with her teachers, failed to complete the assigned readings, and summarily flunked every exam that came before her. When she had attended college several years earlier, she had been a straight "A" student. Now she was failing.

"It seems that I'm failing almost on purpose," Natalie explained. "I've never before had trouble in school." As our counseling sessions continued, this struggling young woman came to realize that she was indeed bringing failure and disappointment on herself.

"Did you kill your husband for the money," I asked, "or was it something you had nothing to do with?" Natalie's face had a startled look. "Well, of course I didn't kill him!" she exclaimed. "A plane crash killed him. I didn't even know we had all that insurance money until after he was dead." I then asked Natalie how long she thought she had to make herself miserable to atone for wrongs that she had never committed. "You just don't understand," she replied. "I feel like an evil person for having all this money!"

As it happened, Natalie dropped out of counseling and continued her self-sabotaging behaviors into the third year of bereavement. Eventually she did remarry and was able to allow herself a considerable degree of happiness, wearing the wedding bands of two husbands. When I met her one day five years later in a hospital cafeteria, Natalie was wearing the white uniform of a registered nurse and reported that her prolonged grief had finally been laid to rest. She had placed the life insurance money in a trust fund for her son's education, and she and her new husband were having to work hard to make ends meet. This was a more satisfying solution to her exaggerated feelings of guilt, she had decided, than flunking out of nurse's training.

Atonement themes occur in the most ordinary healing stories.. After our mother and then our dad died recently, my siblings and I decided to sell some Oklahoma farmland we inherited. It was cultivated wheatland our parents greatly cherished and had owned for a long time. My sister, brother, our six adult children, and I live in five different states. There was no workable way for anyone in the family to oversee the continued farming of that land so far away from us all. I still felt guilty for parting with this farmland against our parents' wishes, even 40 years after graduating college and leaving Oklahoma. I felt a need to show respect for my folks by wisely spending my third of the farm sale income. Especially important was using the money in ways that have brought a lasting pleasure to me and to my daughters and would have pleased their grandma. By turning guilt into positive actions, including setting up a college scholarship in Oklahoma to honor my mother, I now have a sense of peace when I think of my parents

A Suffering "Script"

Some people so expect to be unhappy in life that they bring considerable unhappiness upon themselves. In psychology, this behavior is called the *self-fulfilling prophecy* — that what one expects of himself or herself in the way of joy and sorrow, one plays a significant role in creating.

Person A suffers loss and passes through a difficult mourning period but eventually expects to be free of pain and to resume a productive life. Person B suffers loss, mourns the loss forever, and expects never to be free of pain, never to resume a productive life. Eric Berne, the originator of more comprehensive studies of the self-fulfilling prophecy, would probably have said that Person B is "scripted" to be unhappy. It is likely that he or she learned at a very early age to expect suffering and to fulfill this expectation.

Little children can learn to expect unhappiness from a variety of experiences and environments. If your name is Will and you were named after an Uncle William who was an alcoholic, gambled away his money, and lost his family as a result, you may expect always to be losing out on life. Especially if you look like your uncle and your mother always said you were a troublemaker "just like Uncle William," you may have grown into a troublemaker simply because it was expected of you. As a man now, you expect it of yourself.[4]

Parents make a big mistake by offering up negative prophecies concerning their children's future. When nephew Will was a teenager and came home drunk from a party, the absolutely worst thing that could have been said to him was, "When you grow up, you'll be a drunk and a bum just like your Uncle William!" When young Will lavishly spent three weeks' allowance at an amusement park, a negative parental prophecy would be highly destructive: "You're a spendthrift and a gambler and you'll end up always losing, just like your Uncle William!" The truth is that most young people go through a period of squandering money. Young Will's behavior was innocent, but because it was interpreted as a catastrophic sign, eventually Will himself may interpret it as such.

Parents often believe that such reverse psychology techniques will cause a youngster to "straighten up." They believe that a child will fear and thereby avoid the lasting consequences of nonproductive behavior. More often than not, however, negative prophecies repeated again and again produce negative behavior, sometimes for a lifetime.

Let's suppose that nephew Will is 40 years old now and a genuine crisis happens to him, an unavoidable loss. While he's stone sober, an automobile accident occurs which is not his fault but costs him dearly. He suffers a permanent physical disability.

Normally, a person in this situation would undergo an intensive mourning period for a year or two. He would pass through all the usual stages of grieving: preoccupation with the loss, anger, self-blame, idealization, and the rest. Almost any young person whose physical activity is prematurely and permanently curtailed experiences a slow and painful adjustment process, but he or she heals with time. Not so with Will. Will's grief doesn't run a normal course; his suffering is prolonged for years and years.

"I'll never be happy; I was never meant to be happy," Will tells his friends. His drinking and spending problems, which began long before the accident, gradually worsen. Now he has an excuse to become an alcoholic like his Uncle William. Always he will blame his misfortunes on the accident. The truth of the matter, of course, is that Will learned to expect unhappiness from all the prophecies of doom that he heard as a boy. By now he thinks of himself as *destined* for suffering and dissatisfaction in life.

Will's prolonged sorrow is not directly the fault of either the accident or his serious injuries. In his case, prolonged grief is the consequence of having learned long ago to interpret events as a part of destiny.

Suffering scripts can also be learned from having watched the suffering of close family members, especially our parents, as we were growing up. As children, we learned how to cope or not cope with loss. We learned from the adults who taught us, those whose attitudes and behavior we began to imitate quite early.

Perhaps you are a woman whose mother was unhappily married for many years. You may expect to be unhappy in your own marriage as a result of never having seen your mother truly satisfied in married life. You may stay married to a man who is mean to you, if that's what your mother chose to do. Possibly you will mourn your unhappiness for many years but do nothing to change it.

Although pessimism is an attitude that frequently accompanies normal grief, a gloomy view of life that goes on for longer than two years may be a signal that your life is being dominated by a suffering "script" learned in childhood. You may feel undeserving of a better life, or you may feel that you just were not meant to be happy, or that you are a "tragic figure."

If your life has had a pattern of repeated losses of a similar nature, it is possible that your life is dominated by negative expectations, which you are repeatedly living out. Some people's life stories are tragic because fate has stricken them with one unavoidable loss experience after another. Many others, however, suffer a continual series of loss events, some of which were unavoidable and some of which were not. In general, persons who are "scripted" to be unhappy are those who suffer *avoidable* losses time and again or who suffer a single unavoidable loss but never recover.

Although pessimism and negativity tend to be highly resistant to change, we can learn to expect satisfaction from life instead of unhappiness. The first step is recognizing the problem. If you believe you are "fated" for unhappiness, you can change this belief. Roles and attitudes in life are learned and can be unlearned. You can seek the help of understanding friends or a trained counselor to receive support for bringing about the desired change.

A Fateful Constellation of Events

Margaret, a rising lawyer in her early 30s, came to me for help with the dejected feelings that had surged around her since her divorce three years earlier. As Margaret slowly sorted out her story, she began to realize that a strange order of experiences had colored her responses and shaped her feelings.

When Margaret's husband left her, she did not understand why, since he left without an explanation. She remembered his tenderness toward her during the early part of their marriage and courtship. She cherished the memory of the bouquet of daisies he placed beside her in bed after their first intimacy. The remembrance of her husband's gentleness was especially important to Margaret because of her father's meanness toward both her and her mother and the belittlement she experienced as a young girl at her father's hands.

A tomboy as a girl, as a woman she retained the assertive, athletic, and independent traits she had assumed in order to win her woman-belittling father's approval. But beneath it all, Margaret found it hard to believe that she, a woman, could be loved by a man. Therefore, the eventual realization that her husband was gay and had left her for a *man* was unbearably painful. She was sure her husband had left because her father was right about women — that they weren't worth much of anything. If her father couldn't love her as she was and her husband couldn't continue to love her as she was, she decided she was simply unlovable.

Fortunately, Margaret sought counseling when her husband left and, with the help of friends, found a male therapist in his 50s. He was a warm man who believed in openly affirming the worth of his clients when they needed it. Margaret received her counselor's affirmation, and his affection, purely asexual, reassured her that, yes, she was a woman men could care for. As she surfaced from the depths of her grief, she left therapy.

Yet when Margaret came to me two years later, she was still struggling with depression. As her attempts to establish a successful love relationship with a man other than her husband failed, she again doubted her own worth. As she reviewed her history, Margaret realized that her continuing unhappiness since her divorce stemmed from unresolved feelings toward her father, both her love for him and her hatred. She had long refused to forgive his often cruel and disrespectful treatment of both her and her mother. Until she could grieve the pain and work through the anger caused by her father, she could not recover from her divorce.

A fateful constellation of events had prolonged her grief. Because she felt rejected by her father for being female, it was the worst of all possible events that the only other man she had deeply loved also rejected her because she was female.

As Margaret came to forgive her father, she learned that he had loved her in his own way. She came to realize that her husband had loved her too, that he was a man, though gay, who had ended their marriage out of the conviction that its ending would be best for them both. Had Margaret's husband died or left her under different circumstances, her grief might not have been prolonged for several years. However, when separation came in the form of a rejection of Margaret as a woman, the old unresolved conflicts with her father resulted in a prolonged depression. Her mourning was excessive because her loss struck at the core of her personal history, her personality, and her sexual identity.

With the earlier help of her male therapist and with my counseling, Margaret was able to affirm her worth as a woman. Her mourning period was finally ended. When I last saw Margaret, she was continuing to advance as a lawyer and was enjoying a tender affair with a gentle man who cherished her as she is — athletic, assertive, and capable of giving and receiving love.

Idealization

When our idealization of a loved one causes grief to be prolonged, what is called *positive projection* may be at the root of our difficulties. Positive projection means that we sometimes attribute our strengths to others to such an excessive extent that when the loved person is lost we are left feeling empty and unable to continue.

Two hundred years ago medical examiners were occasionally known to certify "griefe" as an official cause of death.[5] Even today, the expression is heard, "He died of a broken heart" or "She never got over his death and she herself died soon after." In such instances, it is certainly appropriate to feel compassionate toward the bereaved person who finds it impossible to continue living. At the same time, if you are such a mourner, it may be helpful if you understand the concept of positive projection.

Lily Pincus aptly describes positive projection:

> People whose self-confidence has been severely undermined, perhaps from earliest childhood, find it difficult to believe in, and hold onto, anything good in themselves, such as beauty, talent, kindness or love... Such people may choose partners whom they can idealize and adorn with all desirable characteristics, with everything that is good and beautiful, hoping that they can put themselves in touch with what might be good inside themselves. When such a partner dies, he takes all the goodness away with him and leaves the survivor emptied of all that makes life worth living. The bereaved may feel so impoverished that he becomes deeply depressed and cannot

continue to live. He may not even want to live, for only the dead have value.[6]

There are both men and women who have devoted their whole lives to the love partner and, once the partner is gone, they have no life of their own. These grieving persons' status has changed and they must adjust to new roles.[7]

Positive projection, of course, can be a problem not only for those whose spouse has died. The end of any love relationship can be followed by prolonged grieving that is the result of excessive idealization. A bereaved parent or anyone grieving the loss of a family member may attribute to the lost one an embodiment of all that is good.

Idealization is a normal part of the grieving process, especially in the first year. It is only when the idealization is absolute, long-lasting, and at the expense of the bereaved person's sense of self-worth that idealization leads to trouble. As Lily Pincus explains in the story of grief she and her neighbor experienced upon the deaths of their husbands, it was necessary "to take back projections, and all that we had made of them, from our dead partners and integrate them within our own personalities... Otherwise, the bereaved cannot become separate enough from the lost partner to bury him truly, for what has been lost was part of his own personality."[8]

If you projected onto your lost loved one all of your own best qualities, potentials, goodness, and loving traits, you'll need to reclaim those qualities that belong to you.

10. WHEN PROFESSIONAL HELP IS NEEDED

Change can only take place through inner struggle.

— T. I. Rubin

There are many reasons why people seek professional help. Sometimes our friends aren't available to provide the kind of listening and support we need, or we are troubled by the idea of burdening our friends. At other times we decide that therapy will help our grief and healing process to move along more rapidly. Seeking help is not an indication of illness. It's a sign of having the strength and determination to care well for ourselves.

My Story

When a close colleague died suddenly of suicide at the age of 44, I was devastated. At the college where we were both professors, Dr. M. was my best friend. We had lunch together at work every Tuesday and Thursday, then walked together on the athletic track. With other friends we regularly played cards and had dinner at each other's homes. To my daughters, he was "Uncle Al," our sometime companion on family vacations.

As a psychologist I often teach whole courses on severe depression and assessing suicide risk. I was unrelenting in self-blame and furious with myself: "How could I have not saved my own friend's life? Were there warning signs? How could I have missed them?"

As the mother of two little girls (ages 8 and 5 then), I realized that I couldn't just keep walking around the house crying. I kept waking up at night in a cold sweat. In nightmares, I was replaying an ugly suicide scene.

In times such as these it becomes apparent that we can't be our own doctor or therapist. I sought the help of a kind and understanding psychologist. Over a period of months, she helped me mourn and come to understand why I was not to blame for my dear friend's death. Had he allowed me to see the severity of his depression or shared his suicidal thoughts or allowed me to know that he'd been hospitalized before with major depression, I could have helped. My therapist enabled me to see that I related to my colleague as a *friend*, not as a *patient*, so I wasn't looking for signs and symptoms. Had I been reviewing a checklist to assess my friend's mental health while listening to him grieve the recent deaths of both of his parents, I would have been an odd and insensitive sort of friend.

Even after the first counseling session with my empathetic therapist, I was able again to be a well-functioning mom at home. It is not a bad thing to have your children see you cry, but usually it's better to share your more intense emotions with other adults. My daughters were young and needed to go on living their normal, happy lives as children.

Suicide is too big a concept for kindergarten and elementary school children to grasp. I told my girls that their Uncle Al had died of depression. It was an incomplete but truthful statement. Years later, when both daughters were old enough for a broader explanation, I explained the rest of the story.

Seeking professional help is not something you need be ashamed of or have to explain to others. Smart people go to the dentist when they have a toothache and go back for a series of treatments when they need a root canal. Similarly, sometimes professional counseling is what healthy, wise, knowledgeable people do.

A Soldier's Story

Danielle Green-Byrd, a U. S. Army specialist assigned to train the Iraqi police, lost the lower half of her arm in a grenade attack in Baghdad. Later her fellow soldiers went against orders and risked their lives to retrieve her severed hand and wedding rings. "As my master sergeant put [the rings] on my right hand, all I could say was *thank you*," she said, in an interview with *Cosmopolitan* magazine. "After you go through an experience like this, people expect you to be damaged psychologically. But I try to be living proof that some people just move on."[1]

Danielle is sustained by the acts of kindness that remain forever in her heart thanks to the soldiers with whom she served. She is strengthened by the sense of purpose she finds working now for the Chicago public schools and pursuing a Master's degree in school counseling. She says she is mentally strong, having grown up with a drug-addicted mom, and physically strong, having gone to Notre Dame on an athletic scholarship. Most of all, this soldier says she didn't feel the need for professional help because "my husband is there as a constant support." She is fortunate.

Many other soldiers — equally brave — need counseling now or will need to seek professional help years from now, because of the specific traumatic circumstances of their injuries or the horrors of war they witnessed. Others carry unresolved wounds from their childhoods or have fewer cognitive strengths or less physical resilience. Literally thousands will need medical treatment for severe depression, post-traumatic stress disorder, substance abuse, or other conditions. Some people are simply more genetically vulnerable to mental health problems, all commonly triggered by the severe stressors.[2]

Many veterans will need professional counseling because there is insufficient support provided by the military or available at home. It is a long journey for many of them to be able to affirm, as Danielle Green-Byrd has said, "I know that to move out of tough situations, you have to look forward, not back."[3]

A Childhood Loss

You don't have to be desperate or in a terrible crisis to seek professional help. Persistent and nagging uncomfortable feelings often can be relieved by a period of psychotherapy or counseling. Great tragedies are more likely to require professional help because the wake is high after an enormous ship passes. But so can smaller tragedies and ordinary problems in living be followed by uneasy waters.

Many who seek help function well in most situations and have no major emotional problems. They are concerned with resolving feelings of uneasiness about themselves, and their primary purpose in seeking help is to grow in self-esteem and self-confidence. Others are concerned with resolving specific conflicts or fears pertaining to work, school, parenthood, an important love relationship, or old emotional injuries carried from childhood into adult life.

Katherine was a happily married woman with three sons whom she greatly enjoyed. She had a part-time job that she liked and was the kind of person almost anyone would have recognized as well-adjusted. After attending a public lecture on the subject of childhood neglect, Katherine phoned me for a counseling appointment. Her alcoholic father had been dead for eight years, she reported. Although he stopped drinking several years before he died, Katherine said that she had never forgiven him for the childhood hurt his drinking had caused her. "I'm 42 years old,"

Katherine explained, "and I would feel happier not to go on being angry at my father for the rest of my life." The lecture she had heard had prompted Katherine to reflect on these things. She wanted to come for therapy "just for a while," she said, "only to make peace with my feelings that Dad never loved me."

Katherine's decision to seek professional help was without a sense of urgency. Her husband was a loving and giving man who had already more than restored her sense of confidence as a lovable person who had been undermined by her father. No significant current problems existed in her family or in her work situation. Thus, once a week for a few months, Katherine talked with me primarily about her growing-up years, her dad's drinking, and her feelings of regret that she had never been close to him. She mourned what never was and, when she was finished mourning, she began to remember several precious events long forgotten. There had indeed been times, Katherine realized, when her dad showed love and caring toward her in the limited ways that he knew. Katherine was comforted by this realization and soon after she terminated therapy.

Too Much Crisis All at Once

Often the circumstances and timing of a loss intensify its gravity. When too many losses occur within a relatively short period of time, within several months or a year, not uncommonly we're in for emotional trouble.

A friend of mine was emotionally strong enough to forgive herself her birth control failure pregnancy and subsequent abortion, was capable of coping with the abrupt end of her love relationship with the man involved, and was capable of handling all the pressures of her advanced medical training. But not all that, all at once. The dramatic hormonal changes of her terminated pregnancy contributed to an engulfing depression. She began to grieve again her husband's abandonment of her years before. Eventually this young woman doctor returned for some sessions with her former psychiatrist. She was suffering too much vulnerability at one time.

Matina was 22 years old and had had ten plastic surgery operations as a result of a severe burn injury as a youngster. Through a dozen years of surgical procedures, she had kept alive her hope of having a face without scars. Actually, she was an attractive woman whose scars were not immediately obvious, but to Matina they were a source of constant self-consciousness. When all possible corrective surgery was complete, Matina was greatly distraught. She no longer had her father's nose. She no longer favored either of her parents in facial features. Her sorrow was very real. "I'm not what God made me," she protested.

About the same time that Matina realized that no more restorative surgery was possible, her parents divorced and each parent immediately remarried. Since her parents' separation, she had been living with her mother in the home where she was reared. Now she had the choice of moving to a new home with her mother and stepfather or staying in the old home with her father and a stepmother only a few years older than herself. Getting an apartment of her own was impossible; she had just begun a new job with a salary inadequate to support herself. It was too much to deal with all at once. Matina sought the help of a mental health counselor to see her through the difficult period.

A Traumatic Loss

According to Edwin Schneidman, "Some losses are more stigmatizing or traumatic than others: murder, a loss resulting from the negligence of oneself or some other person, or suicide. Survivor-victims of such deaths are invaded by an unhealthy complex of disturbing emotions: shame, guilt, hatred, and perplexity."[4] A similar onslaught of disturbing emotions usually invades the person who has been raped and the person who has witnessed a violent death. If you have experienced one of these losses, it's important for you to know that your loss frequently leads to a need for professional help. So great is the trauma and so profound can become one's preoccupation with violence and death or self-punishment, that receiving skillful caring from others often becomes a matter of urgency. If a loved one of yours has been murdered or died by suicide, if your direct negligence caused a death or someone else's direct negligence caused a loved one to die, or if you've been raped or seen a violent death, it's best to talk with a professional person. It's also important to obtain a complete medical examination. Many who suffer such traumatic loss also suffer a decline in their physical health. Of course, any loss can be traumatic and you must be the final judge of your need for help.

A 30-year-old college student of mine handed in a term paper that sent up red flags as I read it. Tara described a day in her life as a teenager, always on the edge of terrible arguments between her parents. On a particular day, when she was 15, her parents quarreled with unusual fury. Angry and afraid, she managed to lock her violent father out of the house. He was furious and loudly threatened that he would kill himself. Impulsively, she spoke back to her father, matching his threat with a dare. "Then why don't you just go ahead and kill yourself?" she yelled. He died of self-inflicted gunshot wounds several hours later.

She was a quiet, frail, undernourished-looking young woman who always sat in the back row of the classroom. She wondered why she always seemed to fall in love with men who would hurt and abuse her. I remember feeling angry at someone's father who would leave it to a tenth grader to take on herself the blame for his suicide. Even her mother assigned the blame to Tara. Many innocent victim-survivors of suicides punish themselves for their "crimes," even without the invitations to self-punishment that Tara received.

I phrased my written response to this young woman's term paper very carefully. "Tara," I wrote, as if speaking in a soft voice, "sometimes a loss is so difficult to live with just because of the *kind* of loss it is, that professional help is needed. Please don't think I'm telling you that you're 'crazy,' because I'm not saying that. Your father's death happened in a way that would give *anyone* long-standing trouble. And you don't have to carry that pain forever..."

Tara went into therapy with a former colleague of mine, a pastoral counselor. His office, I later discovered, was within shouting range of the cemetery where her father was buried. In her paper she had written that she had not been able to bring herself to go near there in 15 years. That was another clue to me, along with the traumatic circumstances of her father's death, that professional counseling was called for. I hoped she would yearn to yell out the window at him her fury for being robbed of a father.

With the help of Reverend Carson, Tara went through a delayed but intense mourning process, struggling with feelings of guilt, shame, and anger that had intermittently plagued her for 15 years. She began to see that her dreadful eating and sleeping habits were a means of self-punishment, as were her repeated affairs with abusive men. Reverend Carson tried to make it clear to her, she told me, that her father's suicide was his own choice and not the fault of a deeply distressed young girl's impulsive words.

Tara seemed only to need a few months of therapy to resolve the anguish she had carried so long. When she met me on campus more than a year later, she had gained weight and her face was not so thin and drawn. "I sat on the grass by Dad's grave the other day," she said proudly. "And I felt at peace with him."

Unspeakable Grief

Doug was a man in his early 30s who struggled with feelings of shame and guilt. He couldn't have talked with anyone but a professional helper. Most other people would have been shocked by his story and would have reacted in a way that would give him further pain.

From the age of 11 to 13, Doug had a sexual relationship with his younger sister. Now that he was older, Doug was greatly concerned that his behavior as an adolescent had permanently damaged his sister psychologically. He had never before told anyone about what had occurred, nor had he shared his anguish, shame, and feelings of remorse. So great was Doug's fear of condemnation that he could hardly bring himself to share his story with anyone at all.

Had I been working in counseling with Doug's sister, I probably would have helped her to explore feelings of anger toward her older brother. Most likely she was psychologically scarred and she would need the opportunity to ventilate feelings of fury. But Doug, not his sister, came for help. It was my place to respond with compassion and to help him understand and forgive himself.

I asked Doug what was going on in his family when he was 11 years old. "Was your father an alcoholic by this time or did that come later?"

My question prompted Doug to recall his father's angry and violent tirades under the influence of alcohol. His father was drinking heavily then, he remembered. "I was terrified of him and hated him," Doug explained. "I would do anything secretly to fight back at the way he pushed us around and humiliated us. But I had to be careful because he'd beat us if he knew it was one of us kids who made his shoes disappear or if he knew we did the other things we did to get back at him."

As the picture was presented of Doug's childhood and adolescence with four younger sisters, an alcoholic father, and a mother who was cold and distant, I began to wonder where young Doug found the human warmth that a youngster needs. "Was anybody in the family ever affectionate and loving toward you?" I asked.

"Nobody but my sisters," Doug responded, with a look of surprise on his face. "Uh, you know," he continued, "I was never rough with Andrea. While all that sexual stuff was going on, I was never mean to her or rough."

"That eleven-year-old boy," I wondered aloud, "he was awfully lonely and desperate for human warmth and contact, wasn't he?"

Doug bent over and put his head between his knees. "I feel so ashamed," he said, almost weeping. "I shouldn't have done it. I should have known better. If I needed closeness I should have found it someplace else!"

"Well," I said, feeling solemn over Doug's embarrassment, "that's easy for a 32-year-old man to say. You were a boy then. You thought like a troubled boy, you acted like a troubled boy, you were a troubled boy. Do you understand what I mean?"

"No," Doug replied, "I was old enough to know better. She was just nine years old. I was 11 and 12 and 13."

When I asked Doug how long it had been since he had talked with a 13-year-old boy, Doug raised his head from his knees and his face had a puzzled look. "Well," I explained, "if you're going to say that a 13-year-old boy should have thought like a man, I think you ought to go find a boy 13 and talk to him. I think you'll be surprised to know what a 13-year-old looks like and even more surprised to meet up with an 11-year-old."

Doug decided to accept my invitation to reconsider his interpretation of the sexual events that took place in his adolescence. He did spend time with several young boys. In the setting of a playground where he shared an afternoon of sports with a group of youngsters, Doug learned how young the boys acted toward the girls who were watching the game and how young they were in their interactions with each other.

Some months later in one of his sessions, Doug reported that he had made considerable peace with the past and his feelings of shame. "I'm still very, very sorry it happened," he said. "But I think that both Andrea and I found a crazy kind of closeness together back then, a closeness that we weren't finding anywhere else."

I'm certainly not saying here that incestuous relationships are healthful or good. Great damage was done to Doug and his sister because of these events. The duration of the sexual relationship and its attendant guilt rendered psychological harm to both youngsters. Still, they did in fact occur. All that was left for Doug was to claim his childhood as part of himself, to understand and accept his past behavior and not forever punish himself for having once been a troubled and needful boy. However, he couldn't have done this by himself. Doug's story had to be heard by another human being, one who would not judge or condemn him for what most nonprofessionals would find unspeakably shameful. Doug today is a functioning person who has come out of this experience with depths of compassion rather than having been broken by it.

Finding Professional Help

It is hardly ever a good idea, unless you have no other alternative, to seek professional help from the yellow pages. It's best to follow someone's personal recommendation. Physicians, clergy, university and hospital chaplains, school psychologists, and college psychology teachers usually can refer you to a therapist. A friend or family member who has successfully sought help often gives the best recommendation. Remember that the person you are looking for is a professional who is especially competent in helping persons to work through loss and bereavement. When you ask someone for a personal recommendation, you can explain briefly that you want to find a therapist who has worked with grieving people, people like you. Most people who seek help from therapists and counselors aren't mentally ill; they're people facing problems in living. Many are suffering from loss.

A clinical psychologist is someone with a Ph.D. or Psy.D. who has had extensive schooling in working with emotionally distressed people. A psychiatrist is a medical doctor who, like the psychologist, has received extensive training in working with emotionally distressed people. The main difference between a psychologist and a psychiatrist is the kind of university training each received. The person with the Ph.D. or Psy.D. went to graduate school and the one with the M.D. went to medical school. Most psychologists and psychiatrists completed their internships in a hospital setting.

Both psychologists and psychiatrists work with a variety of human problems, including crisis situations and personality and life adjustment problems and mental illness. Psychiatrists, unlike psychologists, are equipped to deal with medical illnesses and they can prescribe medications. Only in the military and thus far in a few states can psychologists prescribe medicine for depression, anxiety, and other mental health problems.

A pastoral counselor is a minister, priest, sister, rabbi, or other religious professional experienced in counseling. The best-trained and most qualified pastoral counselors, in my opinion, are certified with the American Association of Pastoral Counselors (AAPC). Perhaps your own church's or synagogue's religious leader is a skillful and understanding person who can help you with your grief. A clergyperson who is an able counselor responds to you in a professional way and, after speaking with this person, you will feel more comfortable with your troublesome feelings rather than less comfortable. When someone is well trained in counseling, he or she is not judgmental of human feelings but offers acceptance and helps you to accept yourself.

Psychiatric nurses, social workers, and certified mental health counselors are also specially trained and competent to see you through your long and difficult period of mourning. Many family physicians also have a special gift for working with and understanding grieving people and can refer you to a good therapist.

When a person seeks professional help, usually what is needed is simply the opportunity to talk. A well-trained professional is someone with whom you can share your sorrow, anger, fear, hurtful memories, guilt, and confusion. Therapy sessions can also assist you in making practical life decisions, which will help you to feel better. You may need to seek help only a few times to see you through a crisis, or you may choose to have regular therapy sessions for a number of weeks or months. Many people are helped by talking with an experienced counselor on a regular basis, such as once weekly. If you have strong suicidal thoughts, you need frequent contact with a psychologist, psychiatrist, or your physician.

Some therapists are quite active in the therapy sessions, raising questions and providing you with feedback. Others may speak very little during some sessions, endeavoring to help you through concerned listening. If your therapist talks too much or not enough to suit you, you should say so. No health professional can help you unless you speak your feelings honestly.

It is very difficult, in the beginning, to feel genuinely cared about when you are paying someone to listen to your story. It's a common feeling at the beginning of therapy to feel that "He doesn't really care about me" or "It's just for the money; that's why she's listening to me." If you have these feelings, tell them to your therapist. Many therapists have had psychotherapy themselves and understand such feelings. As time goes on, most people come to feel that the psychologist, psychiatrist, pastoral counselor, or other certified helping person is caring and empathic, even though the professional relationship means that the caring has certain parameters. Part of the problem is that when we are in crisis, our self-esteem is already at a low ebb, so sometimes we misread the professional's personal style as an indication of a lack of caring.

It's important to remember that when you pay a therapist, what you are paying for is his or her time and training. You can't buy the caring. The helping person gives you the caring as a genuine response to you as a person. Caring just doesn't happen any other way.

Rarely will money, or the lack of it, prevent you from getting the help you need. If you have been through a difficult loss, affordable help can be found. You may find it necessary to rearrange your spending habits so that counseling or psychotherapy is possible. Although sometimes psychotherapy is expensive, insurance often covers at least half of this cost. If you have health insurance, you should find out if it covers psychotherapy and under what circumstances. With or without assistance from an insurance policy, help is available to you. Mental health clinics usually charge according to financial circumstances. Pastoral counseling centers, family service agencies, and other groups have sliding fee scales. Good professional help is an investment with lifetime survival benefits. There is relief available for you. Don't be afraid or ashamed to seek the help you need.

Sometimes Medication Is Needed

Most grieving people don't need antidepressant medications; their depression is relieved by the comfort that supportive and loving friends provide and by the passage of time. In the majority of cases, a grieving person's depression is helped by talking out troublesome feelings with a counselor or friend, weeping, pursuing physical activities, and receiving the kindnesses of loved ones. Sometimes, however, the individual's depressed mood is so profound, overwhelming, unrelenting, and unresponsive to external events that a medical consultation is needed. An antidepressant may be prescribed in such a situation, particularly when a personal or family history has shown that severe depression runs in the family. In such instances, the individual's depression may very well be the result of a chemical imbalance. Antidepressant therapy usually is effective in helping people with this type of depression. While it is still necessary to go through a mourning process, the antidepressant medicine will help relieve the more severe depressive symptoms.

This biochemically based depression I have been describing also has been found among a large percentage of depressed stroke victims. In the first several years following a stroke, many suffer a depression that is not only an emotional reaction to the loss of speech, movement, or memory, but also a chemical depression. With such persons, antidepressant therapy has been highly successful and may be prescribed to *prevent* as well as to treat depression in stroke patients.[5]

If you or one of your loved ones is suffering a post-stroke depression or an overwhelming depression that persists without relief and is hindering your daily functioning, it is important to consult a psychiatrist or other medical professional who can evaluate the depression. Psychotherapy or counseling can be extremely helpful to a person who is depressed, but sometimes medication is needed.

11. TIME DOES HEAL — BUT THERE ARE ALWAYS SCARS

In a way I look upon them [the scars] as battle stripes, marks of my fight to attain an identity of my own.

— Lynn Caine

When I first met Tiffany, she was mourning the loss of her father, who had abandoned the family when Tiffany was quite young. Her stepfather's meanness and her mother's acquiescence finally plunged Tiffany into a state of depression. At age 20 she began to realize that her childhood yearning for a sensitive and understanding dad was a dream that would never be fulfilled. The early 20s often are difficult years because of precisely such realizations. Commonly it dawns on us, about this time, that our childhood is over and it won't ever be any different than it was.

Tiffany's grief process resembled a mourning period that might have occurred for a young person whose parent actually died, especially one left behind feeling unloved and mistreated by the parent. Bitterness, regret, and longing were the primary themes, and usually are under these circumstances. Tiffany's grief lasted with intensity for slightly longer than a year. She suffered intermittent bouts of depression for two more years. Had you known Tiffany and heard her describe the extent of her stepfather's ability to inflict pain, you would fully appreciate why her grieving process took so long.

Tiffany and I met at Chicago's O'Hare Airport recently. Since I was changing planes in the city where she lives and works, we arranged to get together. We reminisced about her grieving and growing process as a college student in Michigan 15 years earlier.

"I remember asking you," Tiffany said, "if the pain would ever go away. You told me that it gets less, but that we never forget it was there. I think things would have been harder if you had promised differently."

"Because it would have been a lie?" I asked. I was thinking how glad I was that I had been able, then, to say the right thing, although I didn't remember exactly what I had said.

"Well," Tiffany continued, "I know that it's hard to tell people the truth. But you have to say how things really are. I could deal with the reality because you told me the truth."

Life really is what it is, Tiffany and I agreed, talking as friends in the airport, sharing our separate journeys. One never *completely* recovers from a significant loss; certain emotional vulnerabilities always remain. Most of us wear a coat with some grief in some of the pockets for the rest of our lives. But not every pocket is filled with sorrow, and the coat is supposed to become a lot less heavy the older it becomes.

Sometimes the grief in the pockets becomes a problem. Old grief doesn't just lie dormant and harmless all of the time. On each of the several occasions that I fell in love with another man in the earlier years after my husband and I separated, the old grief stirred around. I was afraid of suffering another loss. There was an exaggerated sensitivity to certain behaviors and traits characteristic of my husband. Usually it was a highly magnified concern. As more years passed, falling in love again wasn't so complicated.

One's perspective can be permanently altered by an experience of loss: it's so easy, thereafter, to imagine catastrophes. Real effort is sometimes required to move against the fear.

Following Loss —
the Fear of More or Still Greater Loss

Beth and Jake's middle son, Jonathan, was a healthy infant at birth. He came down with meningitis at age two months, did not respond to medication, and suffered permanent and severe brain damage. Medical specialists told the family that Jonathan would be with them for only a few years. He died at home, in his mother's arms, several weeks before his fifth birthday.

It's a normal part of being a parent to feel amazed by the extent that one comes to love a child. A little person is so obviously vulnerable, needful, and dependent. It's also an experience common to mothers and fathers even under normal circumstances to worry about the safety and health of their children. Considering the grief with which Beth and Jake were struggling, one doesn't have to stretch the imagination to understand an excessive concern for the safety and health of their other two sons.

Eleven months later and thousands of miles away from home, Beth and Jake, with their sons Mack and David, were riding on a Turkish bus returning to their beds from a weekend of sightseeing. Three-year-old David was worn out from the trip and was hyperactive, as usual, in his state of tiredness. He bounced around on his mother's lap, talkative and seemingly full of energy. Suddenly he collapsed and was completely still. Instantly Beth reached down to feel his pulse. It was a reflexive action. Beth's husband, with Mack on his lap, looked on with understanding.

David had merely fallen asleep. He always went swiftly into dreamland in this way. The same thing had happened dozens of times before. Still, Beth did what she had to do. She could not help reaching for her son's pulse. Jonathan's illness had been heartbreaking; it would be unbearable, the parents often thought, ever to lose Mack or David as well.

When my husband and I separated, I remember saying to a friend, "What if I lose my job?" and to another friend, "I'm so afraid that my mother will die," and to still another friend, "I'm afraid of losing you." I was fearful of still more loss, scared of getting cancer, afraid of losing my grandmother, my parents, my sister and brother, my closest friends, a close colleague at work.

Loss is a lesson in vulnerability; it teaches us that we have no guarantee against having to give up the people and things most precious to us. I was in no danger of losing my job. My parents and other family members were in good health then. Most of my close friends were healthy and young. My close colleague at work had no intention of taking a position elsewhere and leaving the college. Still, these fears remained intense for a number of months, and occasional anxious feelings hung around for several years.

Most people, in protection of their sanity, go boldly about the business of daily living, undaunted by an awareness of the catastrophes that could happen. Grieving people lose this sense of omnipotence and innocence for a time. We never fully regain it.

Reliving Old Losses

We do not easily become desensitized to old experiences. Emotional pain from the past has a tendency to return again and again.

Ms. Chavez, a 50-year-old divorced woman, had a six-year love affair with a man who worked at the same large insurance company where she worked. Shortly after their relationship abruptly ended, a grief-stricken Ms. Chavez sought professional counseling. In the early counseling sessions she talked with me almost as much about the death of her mother and brother as she talked about losing her friend. Her mother had been dead for 15 years and her brother for ten. Not only did

Ms. Chavez describe the events that led up to their deaths, she wept again as if these losses had only recently occurred.

She had chosen to divorce her husband many years before and had never regretted the decision. Mr. Chavez was apparently an emotionally unstable man whose jealousy and insecurity had smothered and intimidated Ms. Chavez. She left him after he began to physically abuse her and the children.

The end of her recent love relationship was unlike the end of her marriage. This man was a tenderhearted person who had treated her with respect and kindness. Without explanation, he suddenly terminated their long affair, leaving Ms. Chavez with no choice in the matter. She suspected that he had ended their relationship because his ex-wife threatened suicide unless he did so. Still, she felt abandoned.

Intense feelings of abandonment after a current loss commonly evoke a reliving of past abandonment feelings. Since Ms. Chavez's mother and brother had both died relatively young, she perceived their deaths as abandonment. "It wasn't right," she cried, "for them to leave me. They weren't old enough to die!"

For Ms. Chavez, grieving the loss of her mother and brother again was a necessary part of coming to terms with the loss of her love partner. By reliving the old pain that rendered her present loss especially difficult to bear, she gradually found some relief from the pain of her present loss. Though the earlier losses were ten and 15 years old, her grief was immediate and genuine.

One of the most astonishing characteristics of grief, as I have experienced it, is this reality that old sorrow can return to me and to others as vividly as it was ever felt. I've thought many times, "Well, now, there, it's finished; the grief is finally finished." Then along comes a situation that briefly elicits an emotional reaction resembling my intense emotion of years ago.

Scars remain. Over the years, whatever strong feelings of abandonment, fear, guilt, hurt, or anger you have encountered may return to haunt you during subsequent times of crisis. This is not to say that your previous grieving process was unsuccessful or that you are a psychologically unhealthy person. The truth is simply that hurtful experiences require a long time to burn themselves out completely.

You may find that you also relive sorrowful feelings during the extraordinarily happy times of your life. Joy and sorrow often take up living together. For example, in the middle of celebrating a special occasion, you may have feelings of sadness and shed tears for a lost loved one. Whenever we experience intense emotion, the memories of past feelings, both bitter and sweet, surge up.

Delayed Happiness

My mother died in Texas two days before my older daughter's college graduation. Amanda's beloved grandma lived long enough to hold in her hands the Indiana University commencement announcement and to prop up my daughter's lovely senior photo on a shelf above her television. I was thankful to have had several days at my mother's bedside before she died and to be there to walk alongside as her body was taken to the hearse that would carry her back to Oklahoma. But the timing of mama's passing was horrible!

The next day I flew to Indiana, where I made every effort to fight back tears and join my daughters and their godparents in giving my daughter the graduation celebration she deserved. As parents, it is so important for us to safeguard and properly honor the milestones in our children's lives. Studies even show that in families with an alcoholic parent, children seem to fare all right if the rest of the family doesn't allow the alcoholic to misbehave and ruin their rituals, holidays, and celebrations.[1] Parenting, like police work, medicine, and military service, requires that at decisive times, at least temporarily, we "just suck it up!"

The day after graduation, both daughters and I flew to Oklahoma for my mother's funeral. Perhaps some day my first-born will get a Master's degree and we'll do that graduation thing over again, *sans* pain and with a freer kind of joy.

This past May my younger daughter graduated from the University of Maryland. Of course I wished Ashley's grandma had lived to see her youngest beautiful granddaughter's graduation photo. There were some moments of sadness, yes. But three years had brought a lot of healing. In addition, having just awarded the first college scholarship I set up in my mother's memory, I felt a sense of peace.

Happy tears fell all over the place for my younger daughter's academic success and the older daughter's, too. I felt and feel such an abiding thankfulness in my heart for both of them.

Some Survival Defenses Become a Way of Life

One of the main problems with being human beings is that much of what we learn in life we overlearn. Dangers of many kinds present themselves and we learn how to cope with them. We may learn too well. One definition of a psychological "hang-up" is an overlearned protective mechanism.

When difficult circumstances produce anxiety in our lives, we employ protective mechanisms in order to reduce our level of anxiety. Melony came to me as a lonely 32-year-old woman who was terrified of her father and older brother. Both had violent tempers and a proven ability to inflict both psychological and physical pain. As a result of having experienced numerous anxiety-provoking situations in childhood, in which she feared being harmed by them, Melony developed a toughness toward others. She learned that if she appeared never to be hurt in the face of mental or physical pain, her father and brother would cease their cruel behaviors sooner than if she cried or otherwise revealed that she was hurting. She also discovered that if she showed no need to be loved by these two significant persons, neither the father nor the brother would have the power to humiliate or embarrass her in the presence of others.

While she wished to be able to enjoy a close and loving relationship, Melony's thoroughgoing defense system against being vulnerable had virtually excluded intimacy from her life. In fact, she had excluded *all* close relationships — both male and female — as a double protection against being mistreated.

While there were many potential friends in the factory where she worked, including men who sought to date her, Melony always managed to terminate these friendships before any significant level of trust and closeness could be achieved. She had overlearned in childhood a means of avoiding pain.

No one is without psychological hang-ups of one kind or another. All of us are at least somewhat comparable to Melony in that we have psychological protective mechanisms that were once necessary for survival but are no longer essential or appropriate. Because our defenses weren't left behind with the circumstances that produced them, they have taken on a life of their own and can sometimes now impair our relations with others and our attitudes toward ourselves.

Melony wanted very much to have close friendships. She also wished to live as a sexual person, capable of trust and love in an intimate relationship. Her protective shield of toughness and feigned disinterest, however, made friendships with persons of either sex practically impossible. Since she presented herself as someone who needed no friends, few were willing to invade her protective shield long enough to discover that she did have a need and a desire for friends.

Most of us have been deeply hurt in the course of our lives. Loved ones have departed. Tragedies and disappointments have befallen us. On occasion we have trusted others who have betrayed our trust. Intentionally or unintentionally, others have hurt us. One of the ways that scars remain is that our view of the world is colored by past experience. Vows made to ourselves years ago such as "I'll never let myself get hurt again" continue to dominate aspects of our lives. By completely closing down the gates between ourselves and further injury, we also close down the channels through which could flow what is needed for our nourishment.

"You've slammed shut every gate that would let in any pain," I said to Melony during one of her counseling sessions. "But neither can anything warm and good come through the gated wall. Probably that's why you're feeling so lonely."

Once we recognize that we have overly defended ourselves against suffering, we can begin to reopen some of the gates. Still there may always be more protective mechanisms in operation than are necessary or healthful.

Battle Stripes

Lynn Caine, in her helpful book for widows, has a bit of wisdom worthy of the attention of any grieving person. "Acceptance finally comes," she says. "And with it comes peace. Today I carry the scars of my bitter grief. In a way I look upon them as battle stripes."[2] Whatever fears and doubts periodically plague you, the scars are a part of you and of your struggle and development as a personality. You needn't feel ashamed of the indicators that arise in proof of the fact that you are a human being.

Most decorated soldiers would rather there had never been a war, would readily trade their battle ribbons for no more war. Still, the soldier can have the satisfaction that he or she did what was necessary, made of the experience what was possible, learned from it, and came back alive.

Pain is the one of the most significant factors that shapes us into the persons we are. Our scars, even those representing permanent injury, are the "war ribbons" that indicate where we've been. They are a part of our personal histories and present strengths. Why should we disclaim them?

12. CUE POINTS FOR EVALUATING YOUR OWN HEALING PROCESS

better

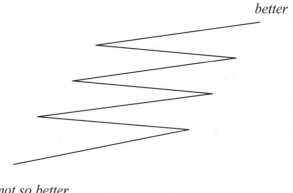

not so better

— Colgrove, Bloomfield, and McWilliams
How to Survive the Loss of a Love

For most of us, the healing process doesn't follow an even course. There are progressions and regressions and there is never a definite date when our grief work is finished.[1] We will have good days, even weeks or months, only to experience again periods of great difficulty. We wonder at times if we will ever get better.

It's not possible to see a child or a tree grow, because the growing happens in such infinitesimal increments. Human emotional growth is like this. Yet there are clear signs that a person is healing.

Usually grief and healing are one and the same process. Our periodic bouts with depression, yearning, loneliness, guilt, fear, anxiety, or anger are part of what is necessary for healing. We know that healing is taking place because we are working through different "*tasks* — actions that must be taken…to recover and return to a fulfilling life."[2] We move back and forth between the tasks of working through our emotions and dealing with the life changes and stressors resulting from our loss.[3]

Grief seldom occurs in distinct and sequential phases. Aspects of one stage often persist into the next.[4] Still, the fact that our grieving process is fluid and multidimensional signals healing. Each person's grief is unique. Each individual has his or her own feelings in the face of loss. Unless we linger many months in a single phase, whether anger, guilt, denial, or preoccupation, the healing process is probably underway. We will become aware that the disquietude of grief is interspersed with increasingly longer periods of calm.

The Ability to Cope with Life

If you are taking good care of yourself in most ways, you can take encouragement in the knowledge that your healing process is underway. The ability to continue one's work, the ability to sustain good friendships and working relations with others at home or at work, the ability to maintain self-care habits, the ability to safeguard oneself from harm, all of these are positive indicators of personal functioning and of the healing process. They are cue points for evaluating your own grieving process.

Sometimes we react to grief with behavior that increases our anguish. We compound our loss by bringing still more troubles upon ourselves. We may alienate our family, jeopardize our jobs, disregard our health, or otherwise intensify our suffering and thus impair the healing process.

One grieving person came for counseling after running up a credit card bill of more than $2000; his compulsive spending was a catastrophe for someone on a grocery clerk's salary. A young woman continually chose highly destructive people as friends and put herself in humiliating working conditions. Still another bereaved person, a man already overweight, gained 80 pounds after the death of his mother.

These are extreme examples. Most people don't deal with a loss by burying themselves in debt, self-destructiveness, or obesity. Frequently in such extreme cases the self-injurious behavior began before the bereavement. For example, those who abuse alcohol during grief tend to have been problem drinkers prior to the loss.[5] So firmly entrenched are negative attitudes and destructive coping patterns that fundamental changes must occur before mourning can follow a healing course. Professional help or a support group such as Alcoholics Anonymous or Weight Watchers is needed to deal with the preexisting problem.

Everybody has some difficulty with personal functioning following a significant loss. Not until considerable time passes do most of us find our "thinking sharper," our "judgment more reliable," our "concentration improved," our "view of the world less self-preoccupied," as described by Colgrove, Bloomfield, and McWilliams.[6] Except in extreme cases, however, healing is progressing even while our ability to cope with life is impaired.

Symbols of Transition

Dorothy, a nurse at one of the hospitals where I worked, was having a difficult time accepting the necessity of her divorce. Dorothy and Paul had tried everything, it seemed, in attempting to resolve their personality conflicts. They had pleaded, argued, tried temporary separations, and gone for marriage counseling. Each partner continued to blame the other. Each behaved as if someday the other partner would change and a resolution would come about. Since neither was prepared to give up the anger, many poisonous verbal exchanges continued to pass between them.

I noticed one day in the nursing station that Dorothy wasn't wearing her wedding band. Paul and Dorothy were planning a final separation within a few months. As a close friend, I wondered aloud what the missing wedding band was saying.

"I've decided not to wear the ring anymore," she said, comfortable with talking about it. "My wedding band is at the jewelry store. I decided to have the diamonds taken out and made into a necklace as a remembrance of the good times. I don't want to belong to Paul, but I also don't want five years of my life to be thrown away."

An important transition had taken place. Dorothy and Paul's anger finally had run its course. Keeping the anger alive, she said, was a way of warding off hurt feelings and denying the inevitability of their separation. They had agreed now, Dorothy proudly announced, to work together on selling the house and accepting the end of their marriage. The whole thing would still be painful, she said, but she wanted to be able to separate from Paul without denying that anything good had ever existed between them.

Being able to take along reminders of the good times while facing the full reality of a loss signals another cue point of healing. We progress slowly but we move in and out of the stages of grief. And everywhere symbols of the transition keep popping up.

"It used to be," said my friend Beth, grieving the death of her middle son, "that whenever I'd catch myself in repose, I'd be aware that I wasn't happy. Every time I sat still, was alone with myself, or wasn't thinking about anything in particular, sorrow was what I would feel. Somewhere along the way there has been a change. I'm no longer feeling that ever-present sorrow. I feel comfortable again in moments of repose. Sometimes I feel very happy."

Harriet Sarnoff Schiff, whose ten-year-old son, Robby, died of a heart ailment, has written a powerful book for bereaved parents. "For about two years," she writes, "I felt that when I cried Robby was close, and when I laughed, I was putting him on a shelf." Eventually, Schiff says, she realized that bereaved parents have a right to joy and that laughter has nothing to do with desertion.[7]

At grief's peak many of us feel very close to a loved person who has been lost. As time passes, usually our reluctance to release that person diminishes. We begin to "develop an inner bond with the deceased,"[8] feel that we have suffered enough and that we are entitled to an enjoyment of life. The changed outlook is a good sign.

There is another reason why many of us resist releasing our sorrow. While grief is intense, we feel especially close to family and friends. Perhaps we fear that the closeness will never again be as rich and meaningful or that our loved ones will abandon us once we are feeling better. As we gradually begin to discover that our family and friends will still be kind to us despite the fact that our wounds are healing, we can more easily begin to move forward. The realization that joy can be shared as meaningfully as can sorrow is indicative of positive transition.

Enjoying laughter, choosing more colorful clothes, paying more attention to events in the news, talking about the loss in a normal conversational tone, making plans for the future, noticing and attending to things that need repair, enjoying things of beauty, being aware of foods that taste good, experiencing one's moods as less fluctuating and more predictable — each of these things too can symbolize healing and an increasing attachment to life.

Learning from the Loss

Nancy, a young woman I was counseling, expressed ambivalent feelings concerning the end of her marriage. When she came for her session one night, I was puzzled by her saying that what she wanted to talk about was how she hated the furniture in her apartment. Nancy spoke with such intensity about the "ugly lamps, ugly sofa, and ugly bedroom set" that I felt she was saying something more significant than the content of her words might indicate. I asked her to play the role of the furniture she hated and speak to me as if the pieces could speak. "I'm Nancy's furniture," she said, assuming the role. "I'm early American, normal, overused, and falling apart. I fit in well here with the décor of the apartment — so well that I have no uniqueness."

Nancy was smiling, aware that she was describing herself. "No wonder I want to get rid of that heavy traditional furniture," she said. "I'm so sick of being normal, proper, practical, orderly, sturdy, and overused!"

She was the oldest child in a large family and had long played the role of the child appreciated and rewarded for her maturity. Even as a youngster, Nancy was always properly behaved, she recalled, more like an older grownup than a child. She made it her business to take care of people, felt "overused" by others, but was always busy maintaining order. Since the age of 14, she had assumed a mothering role toward her friends, her younger brothers and sisters, and the boyfriend whom she eventually married. While she was happy to have a gift for helping others, this young woman felt that she had never really taken the opportunity to be young. In her mind, being "young" meant having the freedom to enjoy life without always feeling concerned about other people and their needs. Nancy told me that she wanted to have some of the fun and carefreeness that she missed as a teenager. She wanted, she said, to go back now and do some things over again.

Nancy's story echoes the story of many divorced women and men who have talked with me. As the healing process gets underway, many are busy clarifying their values, interests, and lifestyle. Feeling that they have overly accommodated themselves to their spouse's choices, they set about to determine the choices they will make on their own. Like Nancy, for example, many women sell the car they chose as a married couple and replace it with a car of their own selection. I did that too after my divorce. New furniture, new hairstyles, new clothing, and even changed diets often emerge. These actions are the symbolic manifestations of a deeper evaluative process. As people heal, they begin to reevaluate their beliefs and attitudes, their feelings toward themselves, their relationships with family and friends. It is a growing process of greater benefit than almost anything many of us have ever done in our lives.

A great deal can be learned about ourselves from an experience of loss, even from a very painful grieving process. Our learning from the struggle is a cue point that real healing is taking place. Every indication of personal growth, every new learning, signifies healing.

The hardest thing is learning some things about ourselves that we don't especially want to know. Growing can be painful. It's not easy to acknowledge that we've made mistakes, wrong decisions and choices, and that some of our suffering may have been self-inflicted. When grief is progressing at its best, we come face to face with ourselves in this way. It becomes clearer what is important in life. Often it becomes clearer that much that is precious in life has been wasted. Sometimes we resolve never to be wasteful again.

Moving Forward

It has been three years since I lost my mother and a year since my dad's death. As in a lot of families, our grief was complicated. All my life I achingly wished my mother could have been married to someone who deserved her, someone able to love as unselfishly and unconditionally as she loved him and all of us. Mama deserved a happier life and none of us earned his mistreatment, disrespect, and occasional outright meanness. There were many good and decent qualities in my father, but he often made his closest family members crawl over an electric fence to find them.

Just recently I took out of storage some of the furniture, dishes, photos, and various little pretty things that remind me of Mama, and I moved them into my own home. Almost daily, sometimes several times a day, I notice these reminders and feel a warmth in my heart. The good feelings are especially sweet when my sister kindly remarks how much it would please our mother to see how I'm enjoying these things from their home. Sometime soon I'll be ready to bring out from storage the horseshoes Daddy tossed on some hot summer evenings on our farm in Oklahoma.

My relationship with my father left many scars. However, as my sister says, we all inflict injury on our children, most of it unintentionally and unknowingly. Regardless, it's important to release the pain, forgive, and move on. Each of us now needs to fully live the life we ourselves are fortunate enough to still have.

Take with you everything good that you can. There is still time to leave your own good deeds and acts of kindness for others to cherish after you're gone.

Integrating the Loss

People don't have to be *victims*, whatever the loss, however terrible it was. Our sorrow can be integrated, can teach us something about ourselves and about life, can be claimed as a part of ourselves. Even horrible losses can be transformed into learning.

Viktor Frankl, the author of *Man's Search for Meaning*, perhaps has taught as many people how to survive loss as any single author ever will. Frankl's experience as a concentration camp prisoner in Germany in World War II is chilling and inspiring. Virtually his entire family was murdered in the Holocaust. Still, Frankl found a way to sustain a sense of personal meaning in life and not to be destroyed by what had happened. Everything precious, including our dignity, can be taken from us, Frankl wrote. But the one thing that cannot be taken away is our power to choose what attitude we will take toward the events that have happened.[9]

At certain times, when the brutality of the concentration camp pressed in on him, Frankl held a fantasy in his mind that gave him the strength not to choose suicide. He imagined himself after the war standing before a classroom of students. In his fantasy he was teaching the students about the meaning that can be found in suffering. Frankl determined that he would take along with him these horrors and that the horrors would be transformed into something of great value. Quoting Nietzsche, Frankl boldly declared, "That which does not kill me makes me stronger."[10]

In our society the word "courage" isn't used widely anymore outside of wartime or other extreme situations. We would do well to resurrect the word and learn to recognize courage in ourselves and in others. Sometimes the one thing that keeps us going is the knowledge that human beings can find the courage to survive, to transform something terribly hurtful or ugly into positive learning and growing.

A woman I know who is in her 40s has already lost two husbands and has also suffered what is called the "ultimate loss," the loss of a child. If you ask me how this woman comes to be the strong person that she is, working as a teacher and making a home for her surviving children, I'd have to say that I don't have an answer. I only know that it's possible to learn from our pain in such a way that our learning becomes useful to ourselves and to others. In the words of author and rabbi Harold Kushner, "We need to get over the questions that focus on the past and on the pain — 'Why did this happen to me?' — and ask instead the question which opens doors to the future: 'Now that this has happened, what shall I do about it?' "[11]

Each individual decides whether and how he or she will grow from an experience of suffering. Perhaps your decision already has been clearly made. Perhaps you've said to yourself, "I am determined that I'm going to learn from my loss." If you have made such a decision, your healing is not just underway — it's a foregone conclusion!

13. FROM OUT OF THE ASHES... NEW LIFE

But today I am someone else. I am stronger, more independent. I have more understanding, more sympathy. A different perspective.

— Lynn Caine

Decades ago when I was a student and it wasn't such a dangerous thing to do, my friend Leah and I were hitchhiking together in Germany, on our way to Austria. We were graduate students with very little money, so there was no choice but to travel with our thumbs in the air. Sometimes, when it was raining, it seemed like a hundred years before we were offered a ride. Leah and I had a lot of time to talk.

As we stood in the rain, soaking wet, watching the passing cars, Leah began to talk with me about a subject quite surprising. "Why don't you ever ask me anything about my parents?" Leah asked. Her voice had an irritating tone.

"Uh, well..." I stammered, feeling very uncomfortable. All of a sudden my outstretched hand and thumb felt very heavy. "Uh, well," I stammered again, "I know that you've lost both of your parents and I thought maybe you wouldn't want me to say anything."

"Just because they're dead, you know, doesn't mean I never *had* any parents!" Leah exclaimed, impatient with my lack of understanding. "Your parents are alive," she said, "but you haven't lived with your parents in a long time either. My parents are as much a part of me as yours are a part of you!"

146

I stood there, my eyes on the vacant highway. I think I felt too ashamed to look toward Leah while she was speaking. My outstretched arms, hand, and thumb felt like plaster of Paris.

"Someday," she said, "will you just ask me what my father did for a living?"

I glanced at Leah's face. Now her eyes were fixed on the vacant highway. "Uh," I responded, "what'd your dad do for a living?"

"He was a rural postman," Leah replied, "and people along his route were always leaving him fresh vegetables or cured sausages in their mailboxes! That was the way poor farm people let him know they appreciated him." She was smiling now and so was I. We talked for a long while about Leah's dad and mom, and I felt very close to my friend in those moments. In no time at all years seemed to pass, the rain stopped, and a European driver picked us up.

At the age of 23, I knew hardly anything at all about grief and about people integrating their losses. I learned as much from Leah that day in southern Germany as I've learned anywhere since. "I have a mother and a father; I will have them for the rest of my life," Leah was explaining to me, without using those exact words. "And don't you go treating me like some kind of orphan, a person who can't take along with me the parents that I had."

Leah's feelings about her parents were not exceptional, but her ability to insist that I respect her feelings was. Usually when others disregard the events of the past that are precious and still present to us, we go along with them without protesting. By not protesting, we play a role in casting aside our own history.

The distressing things that have happened to us ought not be summarily cast aside either. Every experience has shaped us into the persons we now are. What we have experienced no one can take from us, and no one should.

Resurrection

Erich Lindemann studied grief and grieving people for more than 30 years, beginning with the 1942 Coconut Grove fire in which 499 people perished. What "grief work" entails, wrote Lindemann, is finding a way to replace "that which at first seems irreplaceable." We look within ourselves and we look to others — reviewing, scrutinizing, and rearranging our lives — in an effort to replace the irreplaceable. "This is difficult to do because it hurts."[1]

The concept applies whether what was lost was a person, a part of oneself, or a dream. In the case of death, our loved person was unique and irreplaceable. No individual can take his or her place. However, we can find among others various special qualities of our lost loved person. "A number of people take on the life orbit of the one who died," Lindemann noted.[2] Together, these carefully selected others can have an impact upon us that partially fills our emptiness.

"Resurrection" means that our lost loved one is not completely absent, because what he or she had to give remains an ongoing part of our life experience. Among "the network of surviving people," including ourselves, our loved person assumes a new life even though physically dead.[3]

Mourning comes first — the intensely painful realization that what has been lost can nevermore be regained. We suffer longing pains. Usually only gradually do we establish within ourselves the knowledge that what was precious can remain forever alive in new form. It is a reality profoundly comforting: no person or rich experience that has deeply touched our lives ever can be taken away.

If the loss is by divorce, illness, an accident, a war injury, surgery, a fire or flood, infertility, a shattered dream or goal, "resurrection" means that a new life must emerge in some form. In a now classic film series *Begin with Goodbye*, one film deals with a woman named Quinby Schulman, whose cancer required a radical mastectomy. Ms. Schulman found that she had to deal with feelings of being "mutilated and flawed." While struggling with a shattered self-image, she discovered ice skating and new bodily strengths and gracefulness. A social worker before the surgery, Ms. Schulman fully mourned her loss, yet she switched careers, became a skating instructor, and began to enjoy and affirm her body in new ways.[4]

As I was awaiting the arrival of my first-born, an infant daughter who came to me by adoption from India, I met many adoptive parents who described themselves as having gone through a mourning process in giving up their yearning to have a biological child. I personally never felt that way, but one couple who are the parents of two beautiful international children shared with me their past grief over an undiagnosed infertility problem. "What is wonderful now," said one of these friends, "is that we faithfully use contraceptives. If we have another child, we want to adopt, we want another pretty child who will look like our other children." Depending on the nature of the loss, many people, such as the friends I have just described, are able eventually to transform a loss so that they can experience their new life completely with thankfulness and entirely without regret.

What You Have Experienced Belongs to You

When my friend Angela lost her father, her dad's boss came to the funeral home and stood by the casket with the family. It touched me to hear what he said to Angela and to her brothers and sisters. This dear man told the children how their dad talked about them at work. The man's words were specific. He knew very clearly which daughter won the debate contests, which son was a handyman with lawn mowers and any other mechanical thing, which daughter was in high school, which son recently was in the Navy, which daughters had the children and where they lived and worked. Their dad's pride in his family was obvious, the man said. At work, their father "was always talking about his children."

Sharing with Angela these moments was meaningful to me. I knew that in the past Angela had struggled with feeling unloved by her dad. He wasn't the kind of man who was able to say directly to his children that he loved them and was proud of them. Each of the children needed to hear what his boss was saying. At Angela's side I was thinking, "Yes, and each of you can have this knowledge that he loved you and was proud of you. You can have it for the rest of your lives."

A woman with whom I worked in counseling was eight years old when her grandmother died. Kristen's grandmother loved her so well that after 30 years the memory of her grandmother's love was still vivid. In times of crisis she could rely on having dreams in which her grandmother appeared, saying, "I love you, Kristen. You'll get through these troubled times. I believe in you." Sometimes in the dreams Kristen's grandmother would appear as a beautiful bird, flying in the window and alighting on the bedpost. The beautiful bird would then be transformed into Kristen's grandmother. Her grandmother's understanding, kindness, and warmth no doubt will be a comfort to Kristen for another 30 years.

When we lose a part of ourselves — through surgery, an illness, an accident, an act of assault, the loss of a loved one, or the loss of a dream — the persons we are and are capable of becoming must be resurrected in a new form. As we learn something of value from the loss that benefits ourselves and others, our loss is transformed. An event that takes away something or someone precious becomes an event that gives us something new.

Of course it's very difficult even to want to gain from our losses a life that is spiritually and emotionally richer than the life before. Especially early in grief, or when an especially horrible loss occurs, one of the common ways we protest our sorrow is to resist growing or learning from it.

Even if we wished to remain the persons who we previously were, it's simply not possible to do so. Our lives may be permanently damaged by a loss or permanently strengthened. No one stays the same. Each situation is unique, and only we ourselves can search for the answers concerning the changed life and self that will emerge.

Throughout this book I've said that our losses change us and our life course. The reality is unavoidable that one can never again be the same. There is often great sorrow in this reality. Sometimes there is also relief. Thank goodness, I often think to myself, that things can nevermore be the same. I definitely would not like to be the person that I was in the past. While I'm sorry that certain losses have happened to me, I'm not sorry that hurtful events have transformed my life and made me stronger. I've learned too much that's too precious ever to go back again.

One day many years ago I went barreling into my doctor's study with a proclamation. "I'm going to change my name back to Kaiser," I said.

"Why is that?" my doctor asked. She looked surprised by my announcement.

"Well, I don't want to keep my husband's name. I think I should go back to my family name."

We talked for a while about how difficult it can be for a woman with a profession like mine to change her name. Although still relatively young, I had been known by my married name for quite some time. Changing this name would mean starting all over, in a way, so far as my career was concerned.

"But isn't it *his* name," I asked, "and shouldn't I change it so that I'll have my own identity?"

In her quiet and calming way, my doctor just looked at me. Her eyes and words were so capable of reaching inside for the silent questions underneath my spoken questions. "You bought that name with love and pain," she said. "It's your name now."

I couldn't stop crying. I cried tears of relief with Dr. Joffe. I cried in the car coming home. And when I got home that day, I went to bed in the middle of the afternoon and cried some more. "It's *my* name," I kept saying to myself. "I bought this name with love and pain. It belongs to me — the love, the pain, the name — it all belongs to me!"

I've done a lot of healing in the intervening years, despite having some other large losses and challenges. I'm probably as old now as my physician was then. For a really long time, I've been at peace with my marriage, divorce, and former husband. He was a good man and my life is better for all that transpired. I still like carrying my maiden name and his name too. It's who I am and it's where I've been, both of which I can now affirm.

All those events led to my going back to school for a doctoral degree, writing books that have helped more than a million people, and giving talks all over the country on how people go forward after suffering a loss. Most of all, were it not for the end of my marriage, I wouldn't have my two beloved daughters (adopted as babies from India), now young women 22 and 25 years old.

Accepting and affirming the past because of the lessons and blessings we take with us allows us to fully experience and embrace the present. It's what I think it means to "live in the truth."

Life Is What It Is

One of the hardest things to do is release our unrealistic expectations concerning what we feel life *ought* to be. Life ought to be more fair in its distribution of suffering. Life ought not to present choices that are equally painful. Life ought to provide more opportunities to grow through joyous times than through suffering. People we care about ought to be free from sorrows of their own at the times when we most need them. The fact that we try to live good and decent lives ought to result in our not having to suffer any momentous losses. That we've learned so much from suffering ought to spare us from all major hurt in the future. Each of these notions, we learn, is an unrealistic expectation.

Life is what it is. We are all vulnerable and needful people. In human life fairness has nothing to do with illness, death, divorce, accidents, shattered dreams, and a host of other losses. The world cannot be what we want it to be.

We find that as we release our unrealistic expectations of life, space is created for realistic self-renewal. In other words, we begin to recreate ourselves, our goals, our relations with others, our approach to living. Because our expectations of ourselves and others gradually become more realistic, we become less easily disillusioned and more easily satisfied. We realize that life is so much a matter of walking in gardens and learning to recognize that a garden is where we are.

14. Moving Forward: Stories of Hope and Triumph

Fall down seven times.
Stand up eight.

— Japanese proverb

Over the years, through hundreds of hours of interviews, I've had the deeply rewarding opportunity of hearing the stories of men and women whom I've come to call "triumphant survivors." Much of my 30-year career in psychology has been spent studying and writing about these resilient people. What I have learned has changed how I view my own losses and brought me to believe that each of us can overcome fateful events and write our own healing story.

Triumphant survivors are individuals who have endured some of life's harshest and most devastating events yet have gone on to live fulfilling lives. Knocked down by tragedy and its aftershocks, by disappointment and loss, they stand up again and again. When broken by the world, they "grow strong at the broken places" that the great American novelist Ernest Hemingway described in his books.[1]

What follows are the stories told to me by men and women who have rebuilt their lives in the aftermath of crisis or loss. These triumphant survivors were willing to relive painful experiences and share their healing journey — in the hope that you will gain strength, new insight, and the ability to move forward.

Tony: Triumph in the Aftermath of 9/11

Anthony "Tony" Romano was my student in the Police Executive Leadership Program at Johns Hopkins University. From the time I read the first of his many long, soul-searching papers written for my courses, I knew he was a seasoned police officer with a good heart and a lot of powerful wisdom of value to others.

Tony's wife Fran worked at the World Trade Center. On the morning of September 11, 2001, he asked her to take a later train to work so she could do what was usually his job and take the kids to school. This particular morning Sergeant Romano had to drive to Connecticut on police business.

When the news came of the terrorist attack, he was dispatched to the scene. Once there, Tony joined in digging through the debris in search of survivors, eager to help and do whatever was needed. But where was his wife? All cell phones were dead and he had no way of reaching her. Everywhere he saw rubble, dust, and debris. Where was Fran? Had taking the kids to school delayed her normal routine enough to save her?

"People's personal belongings, mostly pieces of paper, were strewn all over," Tony recalled. "Two hundred and twenty floors of offices and not a single desk. Hospitals were expecting bodies, but there weren't any." Hoping and praying that Fran was alive, he kept working.

After five anxious hours, he learned that his wife was safe. Fran was stuck in a train that would have gone to the World Trade Center's underground station. In the train just ahead of hers, many died when the towers came down.

Tony worked day and night. On the second and third days, he helped with the grid search of the crime scene, looked for airplane parts on rooftops and on the ground, and climbed some of the 30- to 60-story buildings still standing nearby. Going from floor to floor, he searched for survivors. Everywhere he saw how people's lives had stopped, frozen in time on dust-covered desktops with open notebooks and unfinished cups of coffee.

Covered in dust, sweat, and tears, Tony and his fellow police officers worked alongside thousands of firefighters, soldiers, ironworkers, emergency service workers, and volunteers. After three days without sleep, he and his fellow officer Eric finally decided to go home to shower and sleep. As they came out through the police barriers, hundreds of people applauded and cheered them. Surprised and deeply moved, he kept his head down.

"Most of my career was doing undercover narcotics work — smashing down someone's door, searching for drugs, threatening deportation. I'd never really been thanked by anyone for doing my job."

Returning to the site in their police car the next day, Tony "recognized the scent of death." Astounded, he asked Eric whether he had showered. Then Tony realized that the smell of death, familiar to him after eighteen years of police work, "was in my nostrils! I couldn't get over this sensation."

At ground zero, they were given respirators, "but it was too hot to wear them," he explained. "The fires at the site burned for months. So you were eating, drinking, and breathing the toxins and eating lunch in a pile of soot with no place to wash your hands." Even five months later, when he walked seven blocks to his police car after an eight-hour day, he found a film of dust on his windshield.

In 2008, as we spent a Saturday together talking, Tony was still trying to make sense of events. Many perished, he recalled, because they complied when told early on, "Stay at your desks. Help is on the way." In the 1993 truck bomb attack at the World Trade Center, the same call had gone out. Those who evacuated suffered smoke inhalation and were covered with soot.

On September 11, many who went against what they were advised to do and listened instead to their own survival instincts fled to safety down many hundreds of steps.

Sometimes we control our destinies. Sometimes we do not. Tony remembered so many fateful stories. A busload of schoolchildren didn't get to the World Trade Center because of a flat tire. An officer's court appearance kept him from regular duty that day. Others lived because they were out sick, on vacation, running late, or subject to some other twist of fate.

How could he — how can we — comprehend this tragic loss of life? The 3000 men, women and children dying — in Manhattan, at the Pentagon, and in the plane that crashed in a field in Pennsylvania after passengers rose up against the terrorists?

As part of a healing process, we all have to find or create a sense of coherence: we have to try to make sense of events, even in meaningless circumstances. When evil deeds bring death and suffering to thousands of innocent people and spare others, it isn't any wonder that finding coherence seems impossible. And the victims of such mass tragedies are not only those who die at the site and their families who grieve them. Their losses are monumental, but they are not alone. Rescue and recovery workers at the scene of mass casualties suffer significant rates of post-traumatic stress disorder and depression themselves.[2]

Extracting something — anything — of value from terrible events can take a long time. Thankfully, acts of human courage, sacrifice, and kindness can transform even the cruelest events. We learn that there is hope for humanity and hope for rebuilding our lives when we experience the compassion of others. We begin to heal when we can learn something from crisis and loss, something that makes us stronger.

Tony lost his close friend, Paul, and other friends and colleagues on that September day. In the five months that followed, he also lost his health. Working in the toxic air and long-burning rubble damaged his lungs and heart. He was just 43 years old when heart surgery and NYPD health requirements forced his retirement. "As bad as all that was," he realized, "there were good things that came out of that for me and hopefully for others."

LESSON #1
Find what you can make better.

Working for five months in ruins of the World Trade Center and trying to take in the magnitude of so many lost lives changed Tony. "It removed me from a position of invincibility and entitlement," he explained.

The youngest of only 12 sergeants leading 3,000 officers assigned to a NYPD Drug Enforcement Task Force, "I was boastful about what we were achieving" and "self-absorbed."

"What happened on September 11 and in the aftermath leveled me, forced me out of the mindset of what I had achieved in the police department and how difficult it was to get there. I'm not that person anymore."

Tony is painfully aware that 300 firefighters and more than 70 police officers died at the World Trade Center. Had his wife gone to work at her normal time that day, she might have died too. These events humbled him, gave him both pause and perspective. "I'm alive. We have our family. We've been fortunate," Tony says now.

In the aftermath, he changed. "I gave up the personal stuff like taking golf trips to Arizona and Florida with guys who had million-dollar homes. I used to be the cop in the pack of guys. I couldn't afford $500 steak dinners, so they would pay for it. My work and my friends were always more important than my family. I was seldom even home for dinner."

A self-described "workaholic raised by a workaholic," he had been harsh with his children, just as his own father had been harsh with him.

Today he has "made a transition from being a selfish person to being a family person." He sits down with his family for dinner because he "wants to hear what may be bothering anyone." He watches his son play soccer without criticism during or after the games. He constantly looks for "better ways to treat the kids and Fran" and appreciates what he once took for granted.

LESSON #2

Your family is the most important thing.

As the debris field became lower, a wooden platform was built overlooking the World Trade Center rubble so that those who had lost loved ones could come visit what had become the gravesite for so many victims.

In mid-October 2001, Tony escorted a grieving father to the platform. He no longer recalls the man's face, age, or appearance, but the conversation they shared still haunts him. "The man was a high-profile financial guy and he'd lost his son there," Tony explained, his voice choked with emotion. "He said he would trade all his wealth, for *one more hour* with his son."

"What was it?" Tony asked, unashamed of the tears filling his eyes. "What had this father needed to say that he could say in one hour? What had he needed to do? Finish an argument or say he was sorry?"

It remains a defining moment in Tony Romano's life. "This guy captured it all for me. It's all meaningless if you don't have what's most important in your life. Your family is important."

"The guy wasn't even asking for his son back," Tony repeated, still moved by the man's sorrow. "I want the people I love to know I love them. I don't want them to live their lives not knowing."

He asks himself almost daily, "What do I want to say to my daughter, my son, my wife?" Then he asks me, "What haven't you said to someone you love that you didn't say?"

Memories are all you leave behind in the hearts and minds of your loved ones.

As the recovery effort continued, Tony escorted other families up the platform overlooking the site where the towers had stood. At the gravesite of their loved ones, family members would cry or pray or stand in silence. "Some wanted to talk. I just listened. I had nothing to say."

Watching those grief-stricken people touched his heart. So, too, did stopping work and standing at attention when a victim's remains were unearthed and carried out on a flag-draped stretcher. Tony constantly thought about what lasts in this life and what vanishes.

"All you have after you lose someone you love are the memories," he realized. "You keep the memories, so they had better be good ones." If something happened to him, he decided, what he wanted for his family "is for their memories of me to keep them sustained."

As Tony has learned, memories of good times, of shared experiences, and of loving words are what last. They mean more to those who love us than any material belongings we may leave behind.

In the wake of September 11, Tony changed his life. Like others who lost loved ones or their health that day, he chose to live the best life still within reach and to help the ones he loved live better, happier lives. He chose not to let his life or their lives be destroyed. Whatever traumatic experiences or painful losses any of us may face, we too have to make such choices.

Lynn: A Cluster of People Helped Her Triumph

Diagnosed with a severe case of Crohn's disease, Lynn was only 27 years old when she had to have an ostomy. She was fitted with a small bag for waste products, worn close to the body and needing to be emptied several times a day. Shortly after her surgery someone from the

Ostomy Foundation came to visit her in the hospital. The visitor was an attractive woman, upbeat in her attitude, who spoke encouraging words. The woman said that she herself had had an ostomy and that it hadn't stopped her from living an active and fulfilling life. To Lynn, the woman didn't look different from any other woman. "I made up my mind," she said, "that the ostomy wasn't going to stop me either."

There were major setbacks. Lynn went home after 56 days in the hospital to a strained marital relationship. Rodney, preoccupied with satisfying his own needs, was grumpy and emotionally unavailable. He was feeling sorry for *himself* because of his wife's surgery and went off for a weeklong holiday with a buddy.

Two months later Lynn, critically ill, was hospitalized for another stay. Her husband rarely came to see her. She didn't know that Rodney had asked her father and stepmother for the key to their summer vacation condo, claiming to be worried about Lynn's health and needing time away. Actually, as everyone later learned, he was having an affair with another woman at her parents' beach house, a woman who was an acquaintance of Lynn's who had recently come to the hospital to cut Lynn's hair! It was a devastating betrayal.

Two weeks after Rodney graduated from the pharmacy school that Lynn had worked so hard to help her husband pay for, Rodney announced that he was leaving her. He admitted to having been unfaithful many times, including during her hospital stay. "I saw no reason to live," Lynn remembers. "I was depressed. I slept all the time. I didn't want to talk to people. I felt sick and stopped eating — a form of suicide."

"I was angry at the disease, angry at the ostomy, angry that I had put him through school and lived with all his promises that we were going to have a house and a family."

Lynn shared with her mom, dad, and sister the despairing times. "I told them I was ugly, a freak, that I had nothing to live for. They said

'You're not ugly. You're not a freak.' And dear old Dad said that some day Rodney would realize he had made a mistake."

"There was a long period when I was pitying myself," she recalls. "I hated myself and felt hopeless. My parents each let me have my feelings of anger for several weeks. Then Dad said, "Knock it off, this is ridiculous!" Lynn's dad later told her he didn't mean to be angry with her but felt it was time for her to start working on getting it together because they loved her. Lynn's mother said the same thing in a gentler way. "It's time to start getting better," she said.

Lynn realized that she was "tearing up her family" by refusing to eat and by giving up on herself. She was shocked by her father's harsh words but touched by his tender ones, and she knew that both themes came from his caring. They were words she needed to hear. Lynn remembered the woman from the Ostomy Foundation who had talked with her about wearing bathing suits and sexy nightgowns, even after her ostomy. Lynn decided, "I'm going to be like her." She began to assume a new attitude.

She received support and caring from her relatives, her fellow teachers, and her high school special education students. Her father, her mother (his first wife), and Doris (his second wife) put aside any differences between them and pulled together to give Lynn the support she needed. She and her sister became close, Lynn says. "Although she is four years younger, she is very motherly to me. It's sweet and sometimes amuses me. She has a heart that is humungous."

Despite struggling with low self-esteem, Lynn risked going on a blind date that her sister arranged. It turned out he was a nice guy, and they married three years later. They have two little daughters now, even though she was told that she would be unable to bear children.

"Now when I go to see someone who has had an ostomy," says Lynn, describing her hospital visits with the Ostomy Foundation's volunteer program, "I wear something close to my body, tight-fitting clothes. I tell them I teach full-time, swim and water ski in the summer, work out at a gym, play racquetball, and write school curriculum. Then I tell them I have had an ostomy and sometimes I lift up my clothes and show them the bag."

Triumphant survivors, like Lynn, are people with determination. They accept support from their loved ones, often seek professional counseling, and — over time — many find the strength to help others who have had similar losses.

Derek and Renée's Healing Journey

Perhaps you or a loved one has suffered a traumatic brain injury (TBI) because of a vehicle-related accident, fall, sports or firearm incident, assault, or war injury. Or you may be suffering another kind of loss that requires a long recovery period and presents challenges for the whole family similar to those faced by TBI families.

Each year an estimated 1.5 million civilians sustain a traumatic brain injury (TBI), the leading cause of disability for Americans under the age of 45.[3] Because of mortar attacks and roadside bombs in Iraq and Afghanistan, the U.S. Army says that up to 320,000 of its soldiers and marines have suffered probable traumatic brain injury.[4] Unfortunately, according to a RAND study, more than half of these veterans with "invisible wounds" have not been evaluated by a physician for brain injury.[5] In all, an astonishing two percent of the U.S. population (six million people) are living today with a TBI-related disability.[6]

Family members who become primary caretakers and those who have been injured often must give up personal plans. You each have your own grieving process to go through while dealing with financial hardships, family challenges, and battling the bureaucracies for Veteran's Administration (VA) benefits or other medical care.

As you read about Derek and Renée O'Neal's journeys, you'll see a love story unfold with much hardship, but with many survival and recovery lessons of benefit to all of us as well.

Sweethearts at Stuyvesant High School in New York City, Derek O'Neal and Renée Stewart went their separate ways through college, marriage and family, military service, careers, and finally divorce. Having never fallen out of love, they found each other again at their twentieth high school reunion. They married the following year and then had a son.

When tragedy struck, Derek and Renée, both 43, had been married for five years. With new jobs, four college-bound teenagers from previous marriages, and a three-year-old son, their good life together was still in its infancy. The accident would threaten every hopeful yearning they had and permanently alter their lives.

It happened on an interstate highway near Detroit, about an hour from home. Derek was driving alone in his car after working late. A deer crashed through his window and struck the left side of Derek's head with unimaginable force. The huge animal was thrown out the rear window as the car hit a guardrail and spun. Derek was left unconscious with his brain severely traumatized and bleeding. His heart stopped beating and his vital signs flat-lined on the highway. Emergency medical technicians saved him.

Hours later, as Derek emerged from the first of three brain surgeries, Renée was stunned by the eerie sight of deer fur still enmeshed in the dried blood of his head and eye wounds. His traumatic brain injury was of a severity akin to that of many American soldiers who have returned from Afghanistan and Iraq. Like them, Derek and his family faced a long and difficult battle for recovery and rehabilitation.

Derek's neurosurgeon told Renée, "You should be pessimistic rather than optimistic. The prognosis is grim." There was only a five to ten percent chance her husband would ever recover, the doctor said.

Renée decided that they were going to prove the neurosurgeon wrong. "Derek was fit, a fighter. I knew if anybody could survive, it would be Derek. I was not accepting that we'd found each other again after 20 years and that just a few years into it, our life together was going to end this way!"

With so many responsibilities and decisions to make for the family's welfare, "I had a very important quality gained from my mother," Renée recalled. "She was a strong woman and I was the same, very focused. I got into the 'zone' athletes get in. I would eliminate all the distractions to do what I had to do."

Renée's college roommate, whose first husband had died from a similar brain injury, was an "angel on my shoulder," and drove with her baby from Indianapolis. Renée asked her friend, "How can you be here helping me when the same thing happened to you, and Michael died?" Her friend reassured her that offering Renée support finally gave purpose to her own loss. It's normal to feel frustration and anger, Renée realized. But she also knew that, "When you get to the place where you can't take it, you've got to accept help."

A shunt drained the fluid from his swollen brain. A respirator did his breathing. Derek's healing was excruciatingly slow. He was in a deep coma for a month and semi-comatose for another three weeks. One day she noticed that his vital signs sometimes improved when she was talking to him or when certain Motown songs played on the boom box she'd brought from home. Renée left the music running when it was time for her to leave his hospital room at night. Even if Derek's cognitive abilities, speech, and motor skills could someday be miraculously restored, she knew they were facing a recovery process that would go on for years. She was determined to try anything that could help him and keep hope alive for both of them.

There were many disheartening times. A person suffering the brain injury usually doesn't remember these early months, but for Renée it was a frightening and exhausting rollercoaster ride. Hope, prayer, her love for Derek, his small advances in the direction of healing, and the kind acts of other people kept her going.

He had Bachelor and Master's degrees in aeronautical science and military arts and science but when Derek emerged from the coma after seven weeks, he couldn't tell a fire engine from a wall clock or recognize his own wife. He even had to relearn how to swallow.

He was a decorated, former Army commissioned officer with over 15 years of active duty, including command of a unit during Operation Desert Storm. It was extraordinary that Derek had begun as an enlisted man, become a sergeant, attended Officer's Candidate School, and retired at the rank of Major. In civilian life, before the accident, he was the vice president of operations for a large automobile holding company. Everything was so different now.

His exposed swollen brain still needed more time to heal before his skullcap could be replaced. Unable to see his head injury in a mirror, Derek was angry about being confined in a hospital room. For a while, he thought he was a soldier again, held as a prisoner of war, and that his wife was cooperating with the enemy. His "escape" attempts ended only when a psychologist ordered, "Major, go to your room!"

Renée was greatly distressed that a medical professional would talk to Derek like he was still a soldier, seeming to play along with his POW delusions. She hadn't been Derek's wife during those 15 years when he was an exemplary military leader. Later she saw the physician's approach as resourceful, respectful, and kind.

At Hope Network Lansing Rehabilitation Services in Michigan, Derek had intensive inpatient, then outpatient, therapy with a multidisciplinary team of medical and rehabilitation specialists that included his speech-language pathologist, Chris Schneider, a Vietnam veteran nurse. Chris helped Derek with his cognitive-communication skills, ranging from attention to memory to word retrieval to problem solving to information processing; she worked with him on conversational and pragmatic language skills. When he moved to the head of the table and helped lead group communication sessions, Chris got a glimpse of the old Derek.

In the three months that followed his seven weeks in a coma, Derek and his wife went to therapy almost daily. "The person who is recovering is the same person, but is different," Renée explained. "I was basically Derek's memory. Every day I came to the rehab hospital and told him about his life. I saw all the deficits but also the tremendous strides. He lived up to the challenge that he wasn't supposed to make it. So whatever happened, we were going to do this together."

The boom box playing his favorite Motown music while he was still in a coma may have laid the groundwork for his strong response to music later on. "Those tunes helped me organize my thoughts, energized me, and made me happy," he explains. "While still struggling to make sense of who I was, music seemed to tap into my memories." Surprised to learn that he had such a nice singing voice, Renée wondered, "Who is this person?" When he returned to Beaumont for surgery to replace his skullcap and sang in intensive care, doctors and nurses came in to listen.

At Hope, they signed him up for music therapy at Michigan State University and he filled the rehab center hallways with singing. "There was a beauty to his voice that captivated the other clients," Chris Schneider remembers. "It was joyous, spontaneous, and uplifting to the staff." As Derek tells it, "I loved singing so much that I even sang on an early outing to the mall. My teenage children gave me immediate feedback on that!"

For those suffering a traumatic brain injury and for their loved ones, there is a very long journey to recovery. "Even two years into his healing, I didn't know how long it would take," Renée remembers. To this day — four years later — he continues to make strides."

"I've had two husbands. I look at it not just as a loss but also as a blessing. The priorities of his life are so different now," Renée explains. "Before the accident, Derek was a Type A personality. He wanted to do his best, make a lot of money, and own a lot of things. Our son was three years old and I would say, 'How much is enough? We need to prioritize.' "

A deer crashing into his car and severely bruising his brain changed everything for Derek in ways similar to how 9/11 permanently changed NYPD Sergeant Tony Romano. As hard as it was to get there over these past four years, Renée unequivocally affirms the transformation. "He's a better husband. He's a better father. Our marriage is better now."

Renée — Moving Forward

Like her husband Derek, René is a "triumphant survivor," as I have come to call those who have triumphed over adversity. She shows others how comebacks are possible. "My life is much more financially insecure than it has ever been," she says, referring to the fact that the couple's income is less than half of what it was before the accident, "but emotionally I'm much *more* secure." Rene was able to move beyond the pain, hopelessness, and discouragement of a life changing personal crisis because she has the trait of learned resourcefulness:[7]

❖ She opened herself to support and advice from others — seeking solutions, hope, help, comfort, and wisdom wherever it was to be found.

❖ She fought to remain optimistic, even in desperate circumstances. She saw the glass half full. At the beginning, at least Derek was still alive, not paralyzed. Though his brain was severely injured, after four weeks he was semi-comatose instead of completely out. Eventually he recognized her and the children. His cognitive function was greatly impaired. While he couldn't distinguish between a wall clock and a fire engine, he *could* read, write, and walk. After several rejections, she finally got him into a cognitive rehab program. Their love was strong. His military training, physical fitness, and educational achievements before the accident were assets.

❖ She learned to live with ambiguity. What would be the lasting impact of his injuries? To what degree would he be able to return to his former life and work? That simply was something unknown, an uncertainty she decided she would learn to live with. "I learned not to wait until we have all the answers," she explained. "Life doesn't always have to be the way you want it to be. We will go ahead and live our lives."

❖ She remained focused and fought against the negative thinking that could have engulfed them all.

❖ She stayed "in the zone," kept busy doing all the practical things necessary to keep the family running and Derek's recovery progressing.

❖ She framed her own view of events: despite tragedy, there was a good life still possible. She was determined to discover, cherish, and be thankful for whatever they could still share.

Derek's New Life

"Trauma can transform or transfix," writes psychologist John Schneider. "But the trauma has to be addressed. The courage to face it, to overcome [one's] fears and the identity loss is essential."[8]

Since the brain injury that nearly killed him and eventually forced him into bankruptcy, Derek says "the three things that challenge me most, right now, are: (1) redefining who I am, (2) being satisfied with who I am, and (3) answering the question that is repeatedly asked of me, and that is, 'What do you do for a living?' "

He went through six months of job interviews. He passed the test to regain his driver's license. But he continued to struggle. He tried working as a car salesman, but forgot what he told customers the first time he met them. Seeing him confused and depressed, René called Hope Network Lansing Rehabilitation Services and asked Chris for help.

Chris asked him to help give a Veteran's Day talk. Next, they prepared a PowerPoint presentation, "The Magic of Music," now given often for brain-injury groups. An inspiring speaker, Derek has found new purpose in his life. He is also enrolled in paralegal studies at Lansing Community College. "I use the resources I have," he says, referring to his handheld PDA.

In a process described by a variety of psychologists, which Ronnie Janoff-Bulman calls *existential reevaluation,* Derek has gained a greater appreciation of the gift of life itself, reordered what matters, seen new possibilities and created new meaning in his life. He has triumphed by gradually constructing a story with a positive ending.[9] Charles Zanor refers to these changes in "successful grievers" as **CPR**:

Character — being tested and growing stronger;

Perspective — viewing life in a new way; and

Relationships — significant others assume expanded emotional importance.[10]

As Derek says, he learned to "to define 'good' as meaning the effect you have on people," that "life itself is what matters." Before the accident, "I was always all about getting promoted and making more money. Now I am so close to my seven-year-old son. Because I don't have a job, I have time to pick Jadon up from school and do things to elevate his life. Many dads don't learn that until it's too late." Gratitude permeates his relationships and provides the "authentic happiness" psychologist Martin Seligman describes.[11]

Today Derek is looking for opportunities to speak to war veterans with traumatic brain injuries to emphasize that help is available and to offer encouragement. His message: "Thank you for your service and sacrifice for your country. You are a survivor and your loved ones are, too. Whoever your family is, your family needs you. That's your new mission. What are you going to do to help your family?"

He is sure of his ultimate goal: "When I leave this earth, I want the Lord to say, 'Welcome, Derek. You have accomplished your mission. You have been the best Derek O'Neal you knew how to be.' "

APPENDIX: COMMONLY ASKED QUESTIONS ABOUT CRISIS

But it takes a whole lot of human feeling
I know from what I've seen
That it takes a whole lot of human feeling
Just to be a human being.

— *Don't Bother Me, I Can't Cope,*
words and music by Micki Grant

For several years I have collected questions from my college students of all ages and from community organizations and other groups where I've given talks on the subject of grief. The questions here are those most commonly asked.

Responding to Others

Q. What is the best way to handle a hysterical person?

A. The word "hysterical" has different meanings for different people. Because of our society's intolerance of strong emotion, people often think a mourning person is behaving irrationally when this is not the case at all. A weeping widow standing over the casket, stroking and kissing her dead husband's face, is many people's idea of a hysterical person. This widow may cause others to experience considerable discomfort, but she is not hysterical. If she were yelling and screaming and throwing flowers about the viewing room, that would be hysterical. It is not hysterical to talk to the dead person at the funeral home or cemetery or to weep to the point of exhaustion.

172

What do you do with a yelling and screaming and flower-throwing person? Walk over to her slowly and say, in a calm voice, "This is very hard for you. Let's go sit down in another room." If she hesitates, call her by name and repeat your earlier invitation in more of a command. Speak firmly in a moderate-volume voice: "Joan, come with me now just for a little while to the other room. You need some time away from here." Take her arm and lead her to another place.

Tears are a catharsis. They express and relieve the intensity of sorrow, guilt, anger, and a lot of other feelings. Rarely do people cry "hysterically." Usually the term "hysterical" is a judgmental label, favored by persons made uncomfortable by intense but normal emotion. Let the person cry.

When the grieving person has cried for some time and appears worn out, you can fix him or her a glass of ice water, a cold soda, or a cup of hot tea. After some calm has come, you can say, "Why don't you come back with me to my house now and have a nap while I fix supper?"

Q. How can you comfort someone who is suffering from a loss in a better way than just saying "I'm sorry"?

A. "I'm sorry" is not an awful thing to say but neither is it a particularly helpful response. A better response would focus not on our feelings but on the bereaved person's feelings. Often we don't know what to say because we don't know enough about the loss situation and how the person is responding. What we can do first is gather information in a gentle way. When a person shows an openness to share his or her inner experience, we listen attentively and we ask questions.

A tennis partner and work colleague of mine lost her father. Several weeks went by without my saying anything to Allison about her loss. Eventually I felt disappointed in myself for avoiding bringing up the subject and not making a point of talking with her. We were about to pass each other, walking in opposite directions, on the campus.

Obviously, in a public situation, this was not the time to ask private questions. So I invited Allison to have lunch with me later on in the day. Once we were at the restaurant, I said to my friend, "I've been wanting for weeks to say something to you about your father's death. But I don't know anything about the circumstances. I don't know if he was sick for a long time or even if you were close to him. If you feel like telling me, I'd like to hear about your dad and how you are feeling."

That was all the invitation that was necessary. Allison and I spent the next two hours talking about her father. Later on I was able to say, "You were so much closer to your dad than to anyone else in your family. It's really hard to lose him. It sounds like you especially feel sad that he died so soon after retirement. You wish so much he could have lived to take the trip that he and your mother had planned."

When I was taking counseling courses in graduate school and working with hospitalized cancer patients at Duke University Medical Center, I told my professor how fearful I was of "saying the wrong thing." Dr. Richard Goodling then gave me a piece of wisdom that I've many times since passed on to my own students in the helping professions: "When people are hurting, they need your help so badly that usually they'll use what you say that gives them comfort and they'll mostly ignore what's less helpful."

You can help by being a good listener. An empathic response is a response that hears the person's anger or guilt or loneliness or worry or shock as it is spoken or implied, and that acknowledges that specific feeling.

Suppose the grieving person has just said something like, "I'm so mad at Aunt Lucy and Uncle John; mother was already in a coma by the time they got to the hospital." An empathic response might be, "You feel furious that your mother's siblings came at the very last. You wanted them to be there while she could still respond. Somehow it feels like they should have been able to get there sooner."

An empathic response focuses on feelings, but only feelings that are obvious or have been openly spoken or implied by the grieving person. It is important not to assume too much about the feelings of one who is mourning, since people have very mixed reactions in a time of crisis.

Q. How would you know if a person wants help in discussing his or her grief?

A. Some people don't want to talk; they don't need to discuss a situation of loss. Others very much appreciate an invitation to talk. We discern the difference between the two by approaching the person with an open-ended statement that can be responded to or brushed aside.

Unless the person is dealing with an especially devastating loss such as the loss of a child or the loss of a loved one by homicide or suicide, saying something like "This whole thing is pretty hard for you" is a nice open-ended statement. "Whole thing" is an appropriately vague invitation. The grieving person can say, "Well, I'll be all right" and convey to you that you've gone far enough. On the other hand, the person can say, "Yes, it really is a hard time for me." Then you can follow up by asking, "What things especially are difficult for you right now or lately?"

Certain people in our lives are largely nonverbal and don't like to talk about feelings. It is unkind and inappropriate to impose on such persons our own expectations that the loss be talked about "for your own good." We should take our cues from the grieving person. If he or she gives indications of a desire to talk, we should respond. Curt, quick responses from a grieving person usually indicate a lack of desire to discuss the loss. Softer, slower, longer responses are more likely an indication of a willingness to share.

What is tricky is that often mourners wish to speak about the loss but realize our discomfort and protect us by not talking. If you find yourself asking a grieving person in a public or busy place how he or she is doing, you might consider whether you really want to hear an honest reply. People don't share personal feelings in such settings.

Your grieving friend, family member, or co-worker doesn't want his or her loss spoken about in a setting that could cause embarrassment. Some people are grossly insensitive in such situations. The grieving person then begins to wonder if the "caring words" show hostility rather than compassion.

Q. If a person is experiencing anger at a loss and displaces this anger on me, what is the best way to respond?

A. "I can really understand if you're feeling angry right now. You've been hurt. I'd probably be feeling angry too. What I can't handle, though, is your putting the anger onto me. It feels like you're giving me the anger that belongs to someone else. Hey, I'm on your side!"

A simple and direct response such as this is usually effective. Your friend probably will come to know that his or her anger is acceptable to you but that you don't want to bear the brunt of it. By using the words "I can't handle..." you state your own feelings without attacking the bereaved person. He or she will be more apt to "get" what you're trying to say if your words avoid triggering a defensive reaction.

Q. We recently had several deaths in the family. My partner and I both lost a parent. Is it possible that emotionally I am not willing to offer her compassion because I am still grieving my own father's death?

A. I'm not sure "unwilling" is the right word. "Unable" is probably a better word for explaining why you aren't more responsive now to your partner's needs. Early in grief, especially during the first six months, it's almost impossible for us to be as emotionally available to others' needs as we may wish we could be. It's important to recognize our human limitations.

You can explain to your spouse that you wish you could be more supportive. Her loss evokes many loss feelings of your own, you can say. Then tell your partner the specific ways that you do intend to be of help and comfort. Explain that while you can't be supportive in all ways, you can assume certain responsibilities as a support to her.

Q. What is the best way to tell someone about the death of a loved one if you are the first to know and must relay the message?

A. Especially if it's a sudden, unexpected death, it's important not to relay such a message by phone. Go in person with your message and express what you have to say simply, directly, and in privacy, "Martha, let's sit down in the other room. I have to tell you something that will be difficult for you." In the private place, you can then say, "Your father died of a heart attack this afternoon. He was dead by the time the ambulance arrived at your parents' house."

Be sure that you or someone else stays with the person after the news has been conveyed. You needn't stay in the same room together for many hours, if your friend expresses a need to be alone. But stay in the same house. If your friend is at work, insist on taking him or her home and say that you will arrange later to pick up the automobile left behind. Your friend will be in a state of shock and probably should not drive herself home.

In those early hours and days your friend can be helped by not having to make decisions alone, not having to prepare meals, shop, or make phone calls. You can run the errands, be the chauffeur, baby-sit the children, make the beds, send e-mail information updates to your friend's close contact people, and watch for other practical ways to help.

Helping a Bereaved Child

Q. What happens to the children in a family when the children lose one of their parents by death or divorce or abandonment? How do they display their loss? How can we help them adjust?

A. Children have vivid imaginations and are often self-blaming in far-fetched ways. Your son, for example, may imagine that his parents divorced or his grandmother died because of some action or thought on his part. He may even begin to misbehave, as if intentionally, in order to be punished for his imaginary crime. Your daughter may imagine that a loved one died because someone expressed anger at the loved person just prior to the death.

If the child has lost a parent through death or divorce, perhaps the child is secretly afraid of losing the remaining parent. This is why it is so important to provide an age-appropriate explanation to a child, even a child of age three or four years, regarding the specific reasons of a loved one's death or absence. In his book *Telling a Child About Death,* Edgar Jackson explains that when a child is not given adequate information, he or she fills in the spaces with fantasy explanations. Imaginary thinking is almost always more injurious to a child than knowing the truth.[1]

To a very young child, you can tell the truth without saying everything. Remember in Chapter 9 how I told my five- and eight-year-old daughters that their Uncle Al died of depression? I waited some years later when both girls were old enough for me to explain suicide. Then I gave the rest of the story. It is important to watch for significant behavioral changes, which may be a clue that the child is misinterpreting the loss or is otherwise having difficulty with it. Children and adolescents often cannot tell us in words what their troublesome feelings and thoughts are. Instead, they show us these feelings through changed behavior.

An active child who normally enjoys the company of other youngsters may begin to withdraw from social activities, spending large amounts of time alone. A typically soft-spoken and easy-going child who becomes a loud and boisterous troublemaker may be crying out for help.[2] Resuming bedwetting or thumb sucking can be signs of difficulty or distress. Nightmares, nail biting, and temper tantrums or problems at school also may signal a troubled child.

Talking about the loss in a truthful and simple way that is geared to the age of the child is the best way to help along a child's adjustment process. Children accept harsh realities more easily than do most adults. Mystery and deception are psychologically harmful to a child; honesty and tenderness bring comfort.

Even an infant senses the emotionally charged atmosphere in a grieving family. The infant in a family dealing with crisis needs to be held more frequently, and routines, such as eating and sleeping, should be maintained on schedule. Toddlers and elementary school children also need the sense of stability that regular routines can provide. They too need to be touched and shown affection more frequently than usual when there has been a loss in the family.

Q. How can you handle a child who speaks of his deceased parent as if the parent were still alive?

A. Children grieve the loss of time and activities once shared with the parent. Someone else now needs to be giving this time and sharing these activities with the child, someone who is a permanent family member such as a grandparent, godparent, aunt, or uncle. The loving and faithful presence of such a person will help the child accept the reality of the lost parent. In addition, the surviving parent can begin to share with the child many of these activities that are now sorely missed.

It is important where and with whom the child is speaking of his dead parent as if the parent were still alive. If the child pretends the parent is alive while he or she is with other children away from home, that is one thing. Many children behave in such ways in order to fit in with other children. Also, if it has been only a few months since the parent died, the child may not have grasped the loss. A child under age seven years has great difficulty with the concept of death. However, if the denial persists and occurs in settings other than have been described here, it is important to get a professional consultation from a child psychologist or social worker or other professional specializing in work with children. Some children need therapy in order to come to terms with a significant loss.

Q. When is a child old enough to attend a funeral? How do you decide whether the child should go or stay home?

A. A child is old enough to attend a funeral when he or she is able to sit through a short service. However, a child should not be forced either to attend a funeral or to view the body of the deceased person. It should be explained to the child that a dead person does not look like an alive person and that people at the viewing may be crying because of their own feelings of loss. Once it is fully explained what a viewing and a funeral entail, the child should be given a choice as to whether he or she wants to attend. If the child chooses not to attend, he or she should stay in the care of someone familiar while others go to the funeral home. The child should then be included in the events of each day by having the wake and funeral described to him or her when the adults come home.[3]

Q. How do we explain our tears to a child?

A. It's important to tell a child that our tears are for ourselves. Small children need to know that we cry because we will miss our loved person, not because something terrible happens to a person after death.

The sadness of yearning for a lost loved one is a natural thing, part of the healing process. Both children and grownups need to know this.

Why We Don't Cry

Q. Why haven't I shed tears over the loss of someone I loved very much?

A. Many men and women, more so men, feel unable to cry. One of the chief reasons is the fear that one's sorrow is "too deep for tears" and the unnecessary fear that crying "might never stop" if it began. More important, when crying has been prohibited or shamed in childhood, it is very difficult to show our feelings as adults.

Crying that is other than a response to physical pain is largely a learned behavior, just as laughing and walking are learned behaviors. As children, we learn about tears from watching the grownups handle their emotions and from watching them react to our emotions. We learn that crying is acceptable to our parents in some circumstances and unacceptable in others. Because some of us learn that tears are almost never acceptable as a response to emotional hurt or even physical pain, we train ourselves not to cry. After years of practice, the training is so complete that it's almost as if one's tear ducts have been permanently closed down.

There are many social inhibitions against crying in our culture, particularly for males. Both sexes in certain occupations such as police and firefighting, medicine, the military, and athletics risk ridicule if they cry. I think it's time for us to allow all people to simply be human beings.

Emotionality has been equated with femininity and femaleness, whereas rationality has been equated with masculinity and maleness. In the minds of large numbers of people, tears are also viewed as an indication of weakness and immaturity.

Still in our society almost anything that women are prone to do more than men is looked upon with disdain when a man exhibits that behavior. This is why "tomboys" are more socially acceptable than "sissies." Girls who like sports and war games are socially acceptable because they are imitating so-called male behavior. Boys who like to play with dolls often are labeled with a derogatory term because they are imitating so-called female behavior. It is no wonder, then, that so many men have difficulty allowing themselves to weep. In this culture, crying is not the acceptable behavior for men that it is, for example, in Mediterranean cultures.

Loneliness

Q. What can you do when you feel you've lost your family by distance, personality differences, unresolved conflicts, or lifestyle changes — and you have a feeling of desolate loneliness?

A. If you are geographically or emotionally far away from your birth family, it's important to establish a closeness with friends that enables friendship to take the place of family. By making a tradition of sharing birthdays, holidays, and other special occasions with friends, you can achieve a sense of belonging.

Sometimes our family members seem very different from ourselves in personality and lifestyle. The family closeness for which we yearn may be unobtainable, even though our parents and siblings live nearby. We may put our feelings into such words as, "I feel that I don't really *have* a family" or "No one in my family really understands me." Often we try to punish our loved ones for not meeting our expectations of them. In anger and disappointment we declare them non-people, non-family, and we secretly blame them for our unhappiness. This mindset gets to be a regular merry-go-round and it's a very effective way of keeping ourselves lonely.

A 25-year-old woman I know, Julie, has a mother who is always admonishing her to get married so she can be "taken care of by a man." Julie is quite angered by these preachments and tells me, "That's an insult against my independence!" and "I don't need a man to take care of me!" Yet Julie's mother is not insulting Julie's independence as much as she is expressing a motherly concern to see her daughter well cared for.

It makes sense to try to recognize that our parents and siblings love us in their own ways, sometimes foreign to our ways. We can accept this caring for what it is or be angry because of what it isn't. Sometimes it's helpful to examine why we are keeping ourselves lonely and playing the role of the homeless child. We can, after all, cease demanding so much that is unrealistic from our birth families and accept the caring that is available to us from these sources.

Nighttime Mourning

Q. If a person has grief dreams and when awakened cannot distinguish if it was dream or reality, is this a part of hallucination or mental confusion?

A. By definition, a hallucination is not something that occurs during sleep except for what is called a "hypnogogic hallucination," that is, seeing realities not actually present just before falling asleep. Hypnogogic hallucinations are common to the pre-sleep experience of many persons, particularly those who are very tired or under stress.

Everybody dreams every night, four to five dreams per night, unless the stages of sleep are interfered with by alcohol or other drugs. You may not think you dream every night, but that is only because you don't always remember dreaming.

The mental confusion referred to in this question is simply that of a person who has been awakened from a dream state or from the deep sleep the follows dreaming. In the early days and weeks of grief especially, the reality of one's loss seems unreal, even when one is awake. Thus it is not hard to understand why a grieving person's nocturnal life may be characterized by the kind of mental confusion described here. Not uncommonly, a recently bereaved person will wake up in the middle of the night and wonder if his or her loss is a reality or only a dream. We strongly wish our loss to be a dream and this desire partly accounts for the confusion.

Denial

Q. What is denial: When is it an unhealthy sign?

A. Everybody uses the psychological defense mechanism of denial. We screen out many unhappy or uncomfortable experiences or realities by ignoring them. Usually it's not something we do consciously; it isn't the same as lying. In an effort to suppress painful reality, we use denial as a largely unconscious mechanism to protect ourselves from anxiety and hurtful reality. Some of us use denial more than others do, but we all have used it from time to time.

A friend of mine lost her father and immediately arranged for her father's brother to be called and told of the death. A family friend called the uncle and said, "Your brother Robert died this afternoon of a heart attack." On hearing the news, the uncle replied, "Well, get him to hospital!" By the time several hours passed, my friend's uncle was able to accept the reality of his loss. He began to make preparations to attend his brother's funeral.

In the normal grieving process at least some form of denial is always present, particularly in an early stage of mourning. To acknowledge and suddenly experience the full impact of a loss is too much for us. We can cope with suffering, without an overwhelming anxiety and without unbearable pain, by allowing the full reality of the loss to come into our awareness gradually instead of all at once.

In extreme cases, the reality of a loss is ignored for months or years. The husband who insists that his marital relationship has never been better while it has long been apparent to everyone else that his wife is miserable and planning to divorce him is practicing denial as an unconscious defense. The same is true of the family member who follows the long-term course of a loved one's illness, insisting all the while that the loved one's health is improving.

Defense mechanisms are our friends — they are protective devices that automatically come to our rescue and shield us from excessive anxiety. The problem is, of course, that a friendly protective mechanism can become an enemy when it becomes a way of life.

Suicidal Clues

Q. How can you determine if another person is a suicide risk to the extent that psychiatric intervention is needed?

A. Professional help is always called for when you see in a person what are known as *lethality clues*. Many grieving persons have suicidal *thoughts* but are not in need of a psychologist, psychiatrist, or other professional helper. When a person gives hint of a specific suicide *plan*, however, he or she is in a state of danger and needs professional help at once.

Contrary to popular belief, most people who kill themselves *do* give advance warning. Adults make wills or give away money and prized possessions. Young people give away digital cameras, iPods, skis, laptops, watches, and other precious belongings. Both adults and young people with a suicide plan tend to drop comments here and there such as, "You won't be seeing me around anymore" or "I won't be here." A highly lethal person commonly is in a state of insufferable anguish or is unexplainably in a good mood following a state of insufferable anguish. The good mood may well be the result of having decided on suicide. Most suicides occur when the person's energy is beginning to return from an anguished suicidal period and he or she has the strength to put suicidal thoughts into action.

When a person first starts to take an antidepressant, he or she may temporarily have an increased risk of suicide. For adults, this is so because the medicine improves one's sleep and energy level right away but it can take two weeks, a month, or longer for their depressed mood to improve. For children and teens, some antidepressants can increase suicide risk. Still, studies show that *not* being treated for severe depression is the number one cause of suicide.[4]

The fact that a person is highly distressed does not necessarily mean that he or she is a suicide risk. The lethality clues listed here, however, are an indication of risk. Distress levels do not kill people, lethality does.[5]

One of the myths surrounding suicide is the idea that people who have attempted suicide before weren't really serious about it and therefore subsequent threats are not an indication of danger. Suicide statistics show otherwise. "Four out of five persons who kill themselves have attempted to do so at least once previously."[6]

Bitterness

Q. You talked about how a person going through the processes of loss was more open to love and to experiencing love. I would like to know how to accept and give love while experiencing the hurt and bitterness of loss.

A. Sometimes it's helpful to say to a friend or love partner, "You know, I'm feeling very bitter. I wish I could feel open and receive the caring you're trying to give me. I wish also that I could be more giving toward you. I'm feeling uncomfortable with being close to anybody, gun-shy right now. But I feel bad about acting this way..."

Such honest talk can help to break down the barriers of misunderstanding between you and the persons close to you. If you are distancing yourself from others, at least these words will help others to understand why. Not uncommonly it happens that once we put into words our feelings about our behaviors and thoughts, the uncomfortable behaviors and thoughts no longer have the same power over us. You may speak to your friend in this way and thereafter find that behaving differently requires less struggle.

It still isn't easy. While we are hurting, it's a natural human response to feel wary of intimacy. Our keen cautiousness has some basis in reality. Attachment to a loved one has led to bitterness and hurt; naturally, we are determined not to suffer further injury. By moving slowly in a new love relationship or friendship, gradually we can regain our lost confidence and trust in human closeness.

Social Withdrawal

Q. Why do people shelter themselves after someone close has been lost? What finally motivates this person to participate in society once again?

A. We shelter ourselves because we are bruised and afraid of more hurt, because we are disillusioned or angry with life, because we haven't the energy or motivation to reach out to others, and/or because we are so preoccupied with our loss that we fear "being a burden" to others. Early in grief we're apt to lose interest in the people and activities we once enjoyed and pursued with keen interest. As we gradually make adjustments to the loss, our tendency toward isolation diminishes.

Usually we are motivated to rejoin the human community when the realization dawns that there is no other way to survive, when the need to be sheltered is overpowered by feelings of loneliness, and when we realize that we are making matters much worse for ourselves by this self-imposed isolation.

Prolonged Idealization

Q. What do you do when you know you have many more feelings to resolve and cannot get past the period of idealization?

A. Six months or a year is not an uncommonly long period of idealizing the lost loved one. Some aspects of the idealization may continue for many years. However, if idealization is one's primary attitude toward the loss event over a period of many months, to the exclusion of other emotions, it may be masking something else.

A problem arises when the grieving person attributes all of his or her best qualities to the loved one. The beloved person's departure thus represents for the mourner a profound loss of self. An individual may give away his or her personhood in this fashion for any of a number of reasons: because one's own personality has never been adequately developed, because self-worthless feelings were firmly rooted in childhood, because guilt feelings toward the lost loved one seem to require atonement for real or imagined wrongs, or other reasons. Sometimes the mourner feels an obligation to idealize and is simply playing out an expected social role.

Prolonged idealization can also result from the fear of confronting more threatening, less socially acceptable emotions. Jason, for example, was a young man whose older sister died in a swimming accident. She drowned while trying to swim in the off-limits lake that belonged to an irrigation project. It was late at night, she had had too much to drink, and she was swimming on a dare from friends. Her surviving brother was secretly furious at her, but he couldn't acknowledge these feelings. "How can I be angry at my sister," Jason told me, "when the price she paid for being reckless was losing her life?" Anger was unacceptable. Instead, Jason turned his anger energy into prolonged idealization. She was his "favorite sister, a wonderful person" and he talked about her virtues and strengths almost constantly.

The first step in getting past excessive or unduly prolonged idealization is to identify the probable source of the idealization. The following questions may be helpful in identifying the likely cause: What disturbing emotions might you be fending off by your preoccupation with idealizing your lost loved person? Do you feel an obligation to idealize in order to receive the approval of others? Are you feeling guilty for past wrongs, real or imagined, and trying to compensate? Are you feeling that you are a worthless person without your lost loved one so you keep his or her memory glowingly alive in order to believe yourself worthwhile? Was a life of your own never adequately developed so that your own gifts and strengths are not apparent to you now? Are you turning all so-called negative emotions into something excessively positive because you feel uncomfortable with anger toward the lost person?

Abortion

Q. I recently had an abortion. Rationally, I know that this was something I had to do, but I feel as though I lost a very real part of me. I find myself wondering what that fetus was. How can I deal with this loss?

A. Women who lose a child by miscarriage or abortion can experience the feeling you describe as "losing a very real part of yourself." Neither of these losses gets enough attention in the media nor among professionals, in my opinion. A part of you *has* been lost, a whole world of new possibility. It would be helpful for you to identify more specifically who or what you feel you have lost. What are your fantasies of the life that would have been? Allow yourself openly to have these fantasies and then to feel sad and/or relieved that what you imagine will never be.

Different women, of course, respond differently to having an abortion. Some women, particularly those with strong religious backgrounds or beliefs, have a great deal of difficulty with feelings of guilt. If you believe that the fetus was *fully* a human person from the time of conception, for example, your guilt will probably be more fierce than if you believe that the fetus was *potentially* a human person.

Especially if you are struggling with feelings of guilt, it can help to share your troublesome feelings with a trusted and understanding friend. Just be sure that you don't speak of the abortion with persons whom you know will condemn you and cause you to become even more upset. Some women inflict a cruel and unnecessary punishment on themselves by announcing the event to those most likely to shame, judge, and condemn. It is not necessary for you to punish yourself in this way. You need compassion and understanding now. If prayer is meaningful to you and you feel a need to ask God for understanding and forgiveness, doing this can be a help to you too.

Since every pregnancy involves a second party, often a woman's feelings of loss have as much to do with the man as with the lost life. You may be grieving the man's response to your pregnancy. Perhaps his response was a disappointment to you. Perhaps your relationship with him feels less secure now because of conflicts between you regarding the pregnancy and abortion. Rarely is a woman able to separate her feelings toward a pregnancy from her feelings toward the man. If your man is sensitive, understanding, and supportive, the degree of psychological trauma that you experience will be greatly reduced. On the other hand, if he is aloof, cold, and insensitive, you may be feeling a double loss — the loss of the pregnancy and the loss of your sense of security in relation to him.

Dramatic hormonal changes take place very early in a pregnancy. The woman becomes more subject to depression, tearfulness, and strong emotional reactions of many kinds. Following an abortion, an immediate and even more dramatic hormonal change takes place. The result can be a period of depression lasting several days or weeks. If your man is not supportive of you during this time, you may feel furious at him or feel abandoned.

It is important for you to maintain a clear picture in your mind of the circumstances that made the abortion necessary. If the pregnancy was not the result of a contraceptive failure but rather the result of carelessness, it is also important for you to examine the psychological motives of your pregnancy.

Healthy Spirituality

Q. Does a person's spiritual outlook play a role in how he or she faces loss, how the person looks at the death of a loved one?

A. In my mind, a healthy spiritual outlook means that the person's religious beliefs help him or her to accept human feelings as human feelings. A spiritually minded person is apt to have, in the immediate and early stages of grief, the same intensity of struggle as any nonreligious person. The only difference is that the spiritually minded person may draw strength from the knowledge that God accepts and understands troublesome human feelings. The person may also receive strength and support from the religious community and strength from the rituals and symbols of a particular religious tradition.

Some religious traditions teach us that emotions such as anger, bitterness, and longing for a lost loved one are inappropriate and even wrong responses to loss. In this case, spirituality is not a help to the bereavement process but a hindrance that confounds one's sense of guilt.

If your religious beliefs have helped you to come to know yourself as a worthwhile person, worthy of God's love and of being loved by other people, your spirituality will almost certainly be a strength for you. Faith is a powerful energy when it represents the trust that, with struggle, our sorrows can be overcome.

NOTES

1. Not To Be Afraid

[1] *Oxford English Dictionary* (1993). *Webster's New World Pocket Dictionary* (1997) uses the word "deprived" instead of the word "dispossessed," but I like the older way of explaining what bereavement is. Laura E. Berk in *Development Through the Lifespan* (New York: Allyn and Bacon, 2007) speaks of grief as "an unjust and injurious stealing of something valuable."

[2] Colin Murray Parkes, "The First Year of Bereavement," *Psychiatry 33* (November 1970), 455, 465.

M. Stroebe and H. Schut "Models of Coping with Bereavement: A Review." In M. Stroebe and H. Schut (eds.), *Handbook of Bereavement Research* (Washington, DC: American Psychological Association, 2001), 375-403.

When people are coping with a loss, what is typically seen is a movement back and forth between feeling the pain and handling one's daily responsibilities and the life changes necessary to go forward, write Stroebe and Schut.

[3] Andrews, Gavin, Christopher Tennant, Daphne Hewson, and George E. Vailliant, "Life Event Stress, Social Support, Coping Style and Risk of Psychological Impairment," *Journal of Nervous and Mental Disease 166*: (1978), 314.

K. Doka and T. Martin, "Take It Like a Man: Masculine Response to Loss." In DA. Lund (Ed.) *Men Coping with Grief* (Amityville, NY: Baywood, 2000), 37-47.

Gender also plays a significant role, as many studies and Doka and Martin explain. Men are less likely to reach out for social support.

Laura E. Berk in *Development Through the Lifespan* (New York: Allyn and Bacon, 2010), 662.

[4] Berk, *Development Through the Lifespan.*

[5] Andrews, "Life Event Stress, Social Support, Coping Style and Risk of Psychological Impairment."

[6] Ronald J. Comer, *Fundamentals of Abnormal Psychology* (New York: Worth

Publishers, 2008), p. 198. After catastrophic events such as the London terrorist bombings of 2005, Comer notes that "hundred or even thousands of people" are comforted by creating memorial sites made up of flowers, candles, photographs, and written messages.

2. Things Will Never Be the Same

[1] Erich Lindemann, "Grief and Grief Management: Some Reflections," *The Journal of Pastoral Care 30* (September 1976), 198-201.

[2] J. Raymond DePaulo, *Understanding Depression* (New York: John Wiley and Sons, 2002), 11-13. "There is a rich, deep feeling in grief, where laughter is shared as well as tears," explains Dr. DePaulo, Chief of Psychiatry at Johns Hopkins University Medical School and Hospital. This is neither the absence of feeling nor the despondency and hopelessness of depression that requires medical treatment.

[3] Peter McWilliams, Melba Colgrove, and Harold Bloomfield, *How to Survive the Loss of a Love* (New York: Leo Press, 1976), 87.

3. Feelings of Guilt and Self-Blame

[1] Edgar N. Jackson, *Telling a Child about Death* (New York: Channel Press, 1965), 51-59.

P.R. Silverman and J.M. Worden "Children's reactions in the early months after the death of a parent," *American Journal of Orthopsychiatry 62*, (1992) 93-104.

L. Dowdney "Annotation: Childhood bereavement following parental death," *Journal of Child Psychology and Psychiatry and Allied Disciplines 41* (2000), 819-830.

Silverman and Worden and Dowdney emphasize that children also grieve in many ways similar to adults. Sleep problems, headaches, low-grade depression, anxious feelings, episodes of crying, and anger outbursts are common.

[2] Colin Murray Parkes, "The First Year of Bereavement," *Psychiatry 33* (November 1970), 455-465.

[3] Gwendolyn Gilliam and Barbara Russell Chesser, *Fatal Moments — The Tragedy of the Accident Killer* (Lexington, MA: Lexington Books, 1991), 235-261.

[4] Elisabeth Kübler-Ross, *On Death and Dying* (New York: Macmillan Co., 1969), 33.

[5] T Tanielian and LH Jaycox, Eds. *Invisible Wounds of War: Psychological and Cognitive Injuries, Their Consequences, and Services to Assist Recovery*, Santa Monica, CA: RAND Corporation, MG-720-CCF, 2008, 492, available at http://veterans.rand.org.

4. Physical Expressions of Loss

[1] Paula J. Clayton, "The Effect of Living Alone on Bereavement Symptoms," *American Journal of Psychiatry 132* (February 1975), 136.

Colin Murray Parkes, *Bereavement* (New York: International Universities Press, 1972).

Laura E. Berk, *Development Through the Lifespan* (New York: Allyn and Bacon, 2010), 660, 662.

[2] Colin Murray Parkes, "The First Year of Bereavement," *Psychiatry 33* (November 1970), 455, 465.

[3] Ronald J. Comer, *Fundamentals of Abnormal Psychology* (New York: Worth Publishers, 2011), 197-203. Also, *Diagnostic and Statistical Manual of Mental Disorders*, 4th ed. (Washington, DC: The American Psychological Association, 1994). Among the symptoms of major depression is a significant weight gain or loss within a few weeks. Other symptoms include a loss of pleasure or interest in normal activities or a distressing depression most of the day, nearly every day and a significant impairment in daily function. Particularly if one has persistent suicidal thoughts, a medical consultation is urgently needed. Severe depression is a biochemical illness and usually can effectively be treated with antidepressants.

[4] Parkes, "The First Year."

[5] Rollo May, *Love and Will* (New York: W.W. Norton and Company, 1969), 150.

[6] Parkes, "The First Year."

5. Anger and Bitterness Can Be a Good Sign

[1] Laura E. Berk in *Development through the Lifespan* (New York: Allyn and Bacon, 2010), 259.

[2] George R. Bach and Herb Goldberg, *Creative Aggression* (Garden City, NY: Doubleday and Co., 1974), 190- 191.

[3] Dorothy Yoder Nyce, "Grieving People," *Journal of Pastoral Care*, March 1982, 45.

[4] Harold S. Kushner, *When Bad Things Happen to Good People* (New York: Schocken Books, 1981), 106-107, 137.

6. What One Gets Is What One Resists

[1] Erich Lindemann, "Grief and Grief Management: Some Reflections," *The Journal of Pastoral Care 30* (September 1976), 198-201.

[2] Elisabeth Kübler-Ross, *On Death and Dying* (New York: Macmillan Co., 1969), 33.

[3] J.W. Worden, "Toward an Appropriate Death." In T.A. Rando (ed.) *Clinical Dimensions of Anticipatory Mourning* (Champaign, IL: Research Press, 2000) 267-277.

7. The Importance of Self-Caring Activities

[1] Helen Singer Kaplan, *The New Sex Therapy* (New York: Quadrangle/The New York Book Company, 1974), 108, 112.

[2] Edward M. Brecher, *The Sex Researchers* (New York: William Morrow and Company, 1969), 155.

[3] Herbert G. Gingold, "Helping Seniors Negotiate Late Sex Life," *The National Psychologist 17* (September/October 2008), 15.

[4] Lynn Caine, *Widow* (New York: William Morrow and Company, 1974), 107, 110, 157, 222.

[5] Alvin Toffler, *Future Shock* (New York: Random House, Inc., 1970) 378.

[6] TH. Holmes and RH. Rahe, "The Social Readjustment Scale." In TH. Holmes and EM. David (eds.), *Life Change, Life Events and Illness: Selected Papers* (New York: Praeger, 1989).

Also CS. Crandall, JJ. Preisler and J. Aussprung, "Measuring Life Event Stress in the Lives of College Students: The Undergraduate Stress Questionnaire (USQ)", *Journal of Behavioral Medicine 15*(6) (1992), 627-662.

[7] Ronald J. Comer, *Fundamentals of Abnormal Psychology* (New York: Worth Publishers, 2011), 154.

[8] *Ibid.*

8. A Slow Readjustment Back to Life and Work

[1] Lynn Caine, *Widow* (New York: William Morrow and Company, 1974), 107, 110, 157, 222.

[2] S. Galea, H. Resnick, D. Kilpatrick, M. Bucuvalas, J. Gold, and D. Vlahov, "Psychological Sequelae of the September 11 Terrorist Attacks in New York City," *New England Journal of Medicine 13* (2002), 982-987.

[3] Elizabeth Kirkley-Best, S. Gould, and W. Donnelly, "On Stillbirth: An Open Letter to the Clergy," *Journal of Pastoral Care* (March 1982), 18.

9. Unusually Prolonged Grief

[1] Lily Pincus, *Death and the Family: The Importance of Mourning* (New York: Pantheon Books, 1975), 36, 128.

M. Stroebe and H. Schut "Models of Coping with Bereavement: A Review." In M.S. Stroebe and H. Schut (eds.), *Handbook of Bereavement Research* (Washington, DC: American Psychological Association, 2001) 375-403.

[2] Erich Lindemann, "Grief and Grief Management: Some Reflections," *The Journal of Pastoral Care 30* (September 1976), 198-201.

[3] Pincus, *op. cit.*

[4] Eric Berne, *What Do You Say After You Say Hello? : The Psychology of Human Destiny* (New York: Grove Press, Inc., 1972).

[5] Colin Murray Parkes, *Bereavement* (New York: International Universities Press, 1972).

[6] Pincus, *op. cit.*

[7] Selby Jacobs and Lorna Douglas, "Grief: A Mediating Process Between a Loss and Illness," *Comprehensive Psychiatry 20* (1979), 165-176.

Andrew M. Pomerantz, *Clinical Psychology — Science, Practice and Culture* (Thousand Oaks, California: Sage Publications, Inc., 2008) 362.

Citing the work of the noted family therapist and researcher Murray Bowen, Andrew M. Pomerantz, in the work cited above, explains that "a primary task for each individual family member is an appropriate degree of self-determination. In other words, healthy families allow each member to become his or her own person without sacrificing emotional closeness with members of the family."

[8] Pincus, *op. cit.*

10. When Professional Help Is Needed

[1] Holly Eagleson, "Wounded in the Line of Duty," *Cosmopolitan* (April 2008), 172-175.

[2] J. Raymond DePaulo, *Understanding Depression* (New York: John Wiley and Sons, 2002), 88-94, 139, 140-41.

[3] Eagleson, op. cit.

[4] Edwin S. Schneidman, "Psychiatric Emergencies," *Comprehensive Textbook of Psychiatry*, II, Vol. 2 (Baltimore: Williams and Wilkens Company, 1975), 1783.

[5] Robert G. Robinson, head of the psychiatry department at the University of Iowa College of Medicine in Iowa City, as told in a recent phone conversation with the author of this book and as quoted by Marilyn Elias of *USA Today*, July 2008. See also: Robert G. Robinson, *The Clinical Neuropsychiatry of Stroke* (Cambridge University, 2006).

11. Time Does Heal — But There Are Always Scars

[1] Daniel Goleman, "Family Rituals May Promote Better Emotions; Adjustment," *The New York Times*, (March 11, 1992). Goleman cites the research of Dr. Steven G. Wollin, a psychiatrist at the Family Research Center at George Washington University.

[2] Lynn Caine, *Widow* (New York: William Morrow and Company, 1974), 107, 110, 157, 222.

12. Cues for Evaluating Your Own Grief and Healing Process

[1] Colin Murray Parkes, "The First Year of Bereavement," *Psychiatry 33* (November 1970), 455, 465.

[2] DA. Lund, "Bereavement and Loss." In J.E. Birren (Ed.), *Encyclopedia of Gerontology* (San Diego: Academic Press, 1996) 173-183.

[3] M. Stroebe and H. Schut, "The Dual Process Model of Coping with Bereavement: Rationale and Description." *Death Studies 23* (1999), 197-224.

Laura E. Berk in *Development Through the Lifespan* (New York: Allyn and Bacon, 2010), 659-660.

[4] Colin Murray Parkes, *Bereavement* (New York: International Universities Press, 1972).

[5] Paula Clayton, Lynn Desmarias, and George Winokur, "A Study of Normal Bereavement," *American Journal of Psychiatry 121* (August 1968), 67-68.

[6] Peter McWilliams, Melba Colgrove, and Harold Bloomfield, *How to Survive the Loss of a Love* (New York: Leo Press, 1976), 87.

[7] Harriet S. Schiff, *The Bereaved Parent* (New York: Crown Publishers, Inc., 1977).

[8] Colin Murray Parkes, *Bereavement, op. cit.*

[9] Viktor Frankl, *Man's Search for Meaning* (New York: Washington Square Press, 1963).

[10] *Ibid.*

[11] Harold S. Kushner, *When Bad Things Happen to Good People* (New York: Schocken Books, 1981), 106-107.

13. From Out of the Ashes — New Life

[1] Erich Lindemann, "Grief and Grief Management: Some Reflections," *The Journal of Pastoral Care 30* (September 1976), 198-201.

[2] *Ibid.*

[3] *Ibid.*

[4] "Mirror, Mirror on the Wall," *Begin With Goodbye*, Film Series, United Methodist Communications; Jeffrey Weber, producer.

14. Moving Forward – Stories of Hope and Triumph

[1] Ann Kaiser Stearns, *Coming Back – Rebuilding Lives After Crisis and Loss* (New York: Random House, 1988). The term "Triumphant Survivors" was coined and the concept first described here, where hundreds of hours of interviews were detailed with people who had overcome all sorts of losses and adversities. The quote "Then some grow strong at the broken places" is from Ernest Hemingway's *A Farewell to Arms* (New York: Scribners, 1929).

[2] John M. Violanti and Douglas Paton (eds.), *Police Trauma: Psychological Aftermath of Civilian* Combat (Springfield, Illinois: Charles C. Thomas, 1999).

[3] National Center for Injury Prevention and Control, "National Traumatic Brain Injury Fact Sheet." www.cdc.gov/ncipc/factsheets/tbi/htm.

[4] T Tanielian and LH Jaycox, eds., *Invisible Wounds of War: Psychological and Cognitive Injuries, Their Consequences, and Services to Assist Recovery,* Santa Monica, Calif.: RAND Corporation, MG-720-CCF, 2008, 492 pp., available at http://veterans.rand.org

[5] *Ibid.*

George W. Casey, Jr., the Army's chief of staff, said on CNN (November 8, 2009), "We have scientific studies that we've just completed that show that after a year in combat, it takes you about two years to get stress levels back to normal garrison levels." The Army's highest ever suicide rate is said to be the result of the repeated deployments to Iraq and Afghanistan whereby troops do not have the time they need back home to readjust.

[6] National Center for Injury Prevention and Control, "National Traumatic Brain Injury Fact Sheet." www.cdc.gov/ncipc/factsheets/tbi/htm.

T Tanielian, LH Jaycox, TL Schell, GN Marshall, MA Burnam, C Eibner, BR Karney, LS Meredith, JS Ringel, ME Vaiana, and the Invisible Wounds Study Team, *Invisible Wounds of War: Summary and Recommendations for Addressing Psychological and*

Cognitive Injuries, Santa Monica, Calif.: RAND Corporation, MG-720/I-CCF, 2008, 64 pp., available at http://veterans.rand.org

[7] John M. Violanti, Douglas Paton, and Christine Dunning (eds.), *Posttraumatic Stress Intervention: Challenges, Issues and Perspectives* (Springfield, Illinois: Charles C. Thomas, 2000). "Resilience," say the authors, "is the process in which the person experiences learned resourcefulness."

[8] John Schneider, *Finding My Way: From Trauma to Transformation* (Old Mission, MI: Seasons Press, 2008).

[9] Ronnie Janoff-Bulman, *Shattered Assumptions: Toward a New Psychology of Trauma* (New York: The Free Press, 2004). Also R. Tedeschi and I. Calhoun, "Posttraumatic Growth: Conceptual Foundations and Empirical Evidence," *Psychological Inquiry* 15 (2004), 1-18. And Janice Romond, "That Is Not Where Our Story Ends: Trauma and Transformation in Potongo," an unpublished paper written as part of her doctoral course work at the Union Institute and University in 2008.

[10] Charles Zanor, "One Way to Handle Grief: Just Get Over It," *Washington Post,* (July 29, 2008).

[11] Martin E. P. Seligman, *Authentic Happiness,* (New York: The Free Press, 2002).

Appendix: Commonly Asked Questions

[1] Edgar N. Jackson, *Telling a Child About Death* (New York: Channel Press, 1965), 51-59.

[2] *Ibid.*

[3] *Ibid.*

[4] Ronald J. Comer, *Fundamentals of Abnormal Psychology* (New York: Worth Publishers, 2011), 246.

[5] Edwin S. Schneidman, "Psychiatric Emergencies," *Comprehensive Textbook of Psychiatry,* II, Vol. 2 (Baltimore: Williams and Wilkens Company, 1975), 1783.

[6] *Ibid.*

FOR FURTHER READING

DePaulo, J. Raymond, Jr. *Understanding Depression*, 2002, New York: John Wiley and Sons.

Didion, Joan, *The Year of Magical Thinking*, 2005, New York: Alfred A. Knopf.

Dodge, Jim, *Not Fade Away*, 1998, New York: Grove Press.

Dunn, Douglas, *Elegies*, 1985, London: Faber and Faber, Inc.

Groopman, Jerome, *The Anatomy of Hope*, 2004, New York: Random House.

Hamilton, Allan J. *The Scalpel and the Soul — Encounters with Surgery, the Supernatural, and the Healing Power of Hope*, 2008, New York: Penguin Books.

Jamison, Kay Redfield, *Nothing Was the Same*, 2009, New York: Knopf.

Kushner, Harold, *When Bad Things Happen to Good People*, 1981, New York: Schocken Books.

Lewis, C.S., *A Grief Observed*, 1961, London: Faber and Faber, Inc.; 1989, New York: Harper Collins.

Livingston, Gordon, *Too Soon Old, Too Late Smart*, 2004, New York: Marlowe and Company.

Neeld, Elizabeth Harper, *Seven Choices: Finding Daylight after Loss Shatters Your World*, 1990, 2003, New York: Warner Books.

Reivich, Karen and Shatte, Andrew, *The Resilience Factor: 7 Keys to Finding Your Inner Strength and Overcoming Life's Hurdles*, 2002, New York: Broadway Books.

Saldana, Theresa, *Beyond Survival*, 1986, New York: Bantam Books, Inc.

Schneider, John, *Finding My Way: From Trauma Through Grief to Transformation by Validating Loss, Trauma, and Discouragement,* 2010, ISBN: 0-9638984-7-7, Old Mission, MI: Seasons Press.

Seligman, Martin E. P., *Authentic Happiness,* 2002, New York: Free Press.

Stearns, Ann Kaiser, *Coming Back — Rebuilding Lives After Crisis and Loss,* 1989, New York: Ballantine Books.

Stearns, Ann Kaiser, with Lamplugh, Rick, *Living Through Job Loss,* 1995, New York: Fireside Books, Simon and Schuster.

Stearns, Ann Kaiser, "Trauma Aftermath — Who is Really at Risk?" *The Maryland Psychologist 48*(1) September/October 2003.

Stearns, Ann Kaiser, "Resilience in the Aftermath of Adverse or Traumatic Events," *The Maryland Psychologist, 49*(3), January/February 2004.

Stearns, Ann Kaiser, "Resilience in the Aftermath of a Traumatic Brain Injury," *The Maryland Psychologist, 54*(3), January/February 2009.

Stearns, Ann Kaiser, "Surviving Job Loss or Financial Crisis," *Link,* Summer/Fall 2009.

INDEX

withdrawal, 39
  social, 187
work, 88–89
  appropriate levels of, 89
  as therapy, 90
World Trade Center, 155, 156

World Trade Center attack (9/11),
  90
yoga, 37
your family is the most important
  thing, 159
Zanor, Charles, 170

About The Author

Ann Kaiser Stearns, Ph.D., is a noted professor of psychology who has received awards for "Excellence in Teaching" from Loyola College, Johns Hopkins University, and the Maryland Psychological Association. Earlier in her career, she was a chaplain at Michigan State University and a behavioral scientist in the Family Practice Residency Program at Franklin Square Hospital. She is a longtime Professor of Psychology at the Community College of Baltimore County (CCBC), and also continues to teach veteran officers at the Baltimore County Police Academy.

Dr. Stearns is the author of "Counseling the Grieving Person" in the textbook, *Pastoral Counseling*; the best-selling *Living Through Personal Crisis* (published in seven languages); *Coming Back — Rebuilding Lives After Crisis and Loss*; and *Living Through Job Loss*. She has authored articles on police officer and first responder exposure to traumatic events — risk factors and resilience — as well as a case study on resilience in the aftermath of a traumatic brain injury, all published in *The Maryland Psychologist*. Another recent article, "Surviving Job Loss or Financial Crisis," was published in *Link*.

She lectures widely around the country and has been interviewed on more than 200 radio and television programs in the U.S. and Canada. Dr. Stearns' 2010 public television special, "Living Through Personal Crisis with Dr. Ann Kaiser Stearns," is being distributed across America and worldwide. Dr. Stearns is the mother of two young adult daughters and lives in Maryland.